LEGAL REVISION AND RELIGIOUS RENEWAL IN ANCIENT ISRAEL

This book examines the doctrine of transgenerational punishment found in the Decalogue—that is, the idea that God punishes sinners vicariously and extends the punishment due them to three or four generations of their progeny. Though it was "God-given" law, the unfairness of punishing innocent people merely for being the children or grandchildren of wrongdoers was clearly recognized in ancient Israel. A series of inner-biblical and post-biblical responses to the rule demonstrates that later writers were able to criticize, reject, and replace this problematic doctrine with the alternative notion of individual retribution. From this perspective, the formative canon is the source of its own renewal: it fosters critical reflection upon the textual tradition and sponsors intellectual freedom.

To support further study, this book includes a valuable bibliographical essay on the distinctive approach of inner-biblical exegesis showing the contributions of European, Israeli, and North American scholars. An earlier version of the volume appeared in French as *L'Herméneutique de l'innovation: Canon et exégèse dans l'Israël biblique.* This new Cambridge release represents a major revision and expansion of the French edition, nearly doubling its length with extensive new content. *Legal Revision and Religious Renewal in Ancient Israel* opens new perspectives on current debates within the humanities about canonicity, textual authority, and authorship.

Bernard M. Levinson holds the Berman Family Chair of Jewish Studies and Hebrew Bible at the University of Minnesota. He is author of *Deuteronomy and the Hermeneutics of Legal Innovation* (1997), which won the 1999 Salo W. Baron Award for Best First Book in Literature and Thought from the American Academy for Jewish Research. He is coeditor of four volumes, most recently *The Pentateuch as Torah: New Models for Understanding Its Promulgation and Acceptance* (2007), and the author of *"The Right Chorale": Studies in Biblical Law and Interpretation* (2008). The interdisciplinary significance of his work has been recognized with appointments to the Institute for Advanced Study (Princeton), the Wissenschaftskolleg zu Berlin/Berlin Institute for Advanced Study, and the National Humanities Center.

Legal Revision and Religious Renewal in Ancient Israel

BERNARD M. LEVINSON
University of Minnesota, Minneapolis

CAMBRIDGE UNIVERSITY PRESS
Cambridge, New York, Melbourne, Madrid, Cape Town, Singapore,
São Paulo, Delhi, Dubai, Tokyo, Mexico City

Cambridge University Press
32 Avenue of the Americas, New York, NY 10013-2473, USA

www.cambridge.org
Information on this title: www.cambridge.org/9780521171915

First published 2008
First paperback edition 2010

A catalog record for this publication is available from the British Library.

Library of Congress Cataloging in Publication Data

Levinson, Bernard M. (Bernard Malcolm)
Legal revision and religious renewal in ancient Israel / Bernard M. Levinson.
p. cm.
Includes bibliographical references and index.
ISBN 978-0-521-51344-9 (hardback)
1. Punishment – Religious aspects – Judaism. 2. Punishment (Jewish law)
3. God (Judaism) – Righteousness. 4. God (Judaism) – History of doctrines.
5. Bible. O.T. – Criticism, interpretation, etc. 6. Bible. O.T. – Historiography.
7. Judaism – History – To 70 A.D. I. Title.
BM729.P85L48 2008
296.3′118–dc22 2008019149

ISBN 978-0-521-51344-9 Hardback
ISBN 978-0-521-17191-5 Paperback

Contents

List of Figures

Foreword

It gives me great pleasure to introduce a little masterpiece of exegesis. Focusing mainly upon a single sentence from the Decalogue (Exod 20:5–6), *Legal Revision and Religious Renewal in Ancient Israel* enables the reader to follow, through all their labyrinthine twists, the thought processes of the biblical authors in their constant rereading and revision of prior traditions. Bernard M. Levinson's hermeneutic decoding is fascinating for its unwillingness simply to highlight the unity of biblical passages, as proponents of synchronic biblical methods are fond of doing, or to identify the breaks and contradictions in these same passages, as advocated by practitioners of the classic diachronic modes of exegesis. Instead, Levinson's method demonstrates that in the Bible the present engages in a ceaseless discussion with the past, which it adapts, corrects, and even contradicts while claiming to transmit it with utmost respect. The exchanges between the present and past are courteous: they follow all the rules of etiquette cherished by the ancients. But behind the formulas of politeness there is often hidden a firm will to reclaim the venerable traditions of the past to bestow their authority upon new formulations required by changing circumstances. In many cases, the discontinuity between the new formulation and the old tradition is obscured by an apparent desire for continuity. Thus, it takes a trained eye to detect, shrouded within the complexity of biblical texts, the subtle play that transforms the recourse to a hallowed past into a powerful means for justifying the innovations of the present. This exegetical method surely can enable us to resolve some of the interpretive cruxes that confront rigidly synchronic or diachronic approaches.

A second point about this book deserves our attention. Commentators often make too sharp a distinction between the composition of the canonical text and the post-biblical exegetical tradition, whether of the ancient rabbis or the church fathers. *Legal Revision and Religious Renewal in Ancient Israel* amply establishes that such a distinction does not stand up to a serious examination of the sources. The exegetical tradition that grew up subsequent to the closure of the canon sinks its roots deep into the biblical text itself. Texts imbued with great authority were reread and modified, sometimes profoundly, to respond to new questions and to legitimize new choices. The tradition could survive only by adapting itself to the present. Biblical authors therefore created a repertoire of tools and strategies that succeeded in transmitting the sacred text in its integrity while also giving it an acceptable turn. The schools of rabbinical exegesis merely received this heritage and developed, adjusted, and refined the instruments that biblical authors had forged long before.

Finally, Levinson teaches us something else that is absolutely essential for understanding the profession of an interpreter at the dawn of the third millennium. His method, inherited from his masters, Michael Fishbane and James Kugel in particular, shows the extent to which an intelligent reading of the Bible is indispensable for understanding our Western culture and the richness of its contribution toward the construction of a more humane and just world. Others have shown that some of the fundamental values of Western law have biblical origins;[1] that, although Herodotus is certainly the father of history, the "biblical historians" have also contributed to the formation of the historical and critical consciousness of our world;[2] and that the Western world's sense of reality owes as much to the Bible as to the classical literary inheritance of Athens and Rome.[3] One should also mention here the obvious importance of the Bible for those who wish to understand art, whether painting, sculpture, architecture, or music.[4]

[1] To the biblical scholars cited by Levinson (J. J. Finkelstein, Moshe Greenberg, and Eckart Otto), we might add the work of the legal scholar Harold J. Berman, *Law and Revolution: The Formation of the Western Legal Tradition* (Cambridge, Mass.: Harvard University Press, 1983); and idem, *Law and Revolution II: The Impact of the Protestant Reformation on the Western Legal Tradition* (Cambridge, Mass.: Belknap Press, Harvard edition, 2003).

[2] In particular, I am thinking of Arnaldo Momigliano, *The Classical Foundations of Modern Historiography* (foreword by Riccardo Di Donanto; Sather Classical Lectures 54; Berkeley: University of California Press, 1990), especially the first chapter, "Persian Historiography, Greek Historiography, and Jewish Historiography," 5–28.

[3] Erich Auerbach comes immediately to mind; see his *Mimesis: The Representation of Reality in Western Literature* (trans. Willard R. Trask; with an introduction by Edward Said; Fiftieth-Anniversary Edition; Princeton, N.J.: Princeton University Press, [1953], 2003).

[4] On this topic, let us at least make note of Jean-Christophe Attias and Pierre Gisel, eds., *De la Bible à la littérature* (Religions en perspective 15; Geneva: Labor et Fides, 2003); Danielle Fouilloux et al., eds., *Dictionnaire culturel de la Bible* (2d ed.; Instruments bibliques;

Furthermore, Levinson reveals the Bible to be close to the modern world through its critical, creative, and innovative spirit. We must perforce admit that the modern spirit does not impose its revisionist interpretations as something external to these ancient texts but rather that the Bible itself introduced and developed the art of innovative reading of which we are the distant heirs. "*Scriptura sacra sui ipsius interpres*" (Sacred Scripture is its own interpreter), the leaders of the Reformation already proclaimed. This saying is true in at least two senses. To understand the Bible, we must first turn to the Bible itself; at the same time, the Bible provides us with adequate resources for its interpretation. In this sense, Scripture anticipates certain contemporary trends in hermeneutical theory, including Jacques Derrida's deconstruction. To be sure, it is necessary to qualify this assertion with important nuances. But it is astonishing to note the close kinship between certain currents of contemporary literary theory and the ways that biblical authors and editors fixed their gaze upon the past in order to size it up, to weigh it, and to deconstruct it before reconstructing it so that it could nourish the present.

The annotated bibliography that accompanies this volume reveals that modern scholarship from the dawn of historical-critical interpretation has been sensitive to the "phenomenon of rewriting at the heart of the Hebrew

---

Paris: Éditions du Cerf/Nathan, 1999); Olivier Millet and Philippe de Robert, *Culture biblique* (Premier cycle; Paris: Presses Universitaires de France, 2001); and Anne-Marie Pelletier, *Lectures bibliques: Aux sources de la culture occidentale* (2d ed.; Instruments bibliques; Paris: Éditions du Cerf/Nathan, 2001). Likewise, see André Wénin, "Des livres pour rendre la Bible à la culture," *RTL* 33 (2002): 408–13.

Bible." From Wellhausen (1878) and Seeligmann (1948) to Veijola (2004) and Carr (2005), numerous authors have highlighted the presence of exegesis within the canon and have studied its chief characteristics. These pages on the history of research into this subject will provide interpreters with quite a useful map, enabling them to retrace the exact itinerary followed by specialists in this field. I wish readers as much pleasure in traveling through this book as I had myself.

Jean Louis Ska, S. J.
Professor of Old Testament Interpretation
Pontifical Biblical Institute, Rome

Preface

I write this preface on a sunny afternoon in beautifully forested Grunewald, a western suburb of Berlin, on *der Tag der deutschen Einheit*, the Day of German Unity, which celebrates the country's reunification, sixteen years after the wall came down. A scant hundred and fifty yards down Königsallee, the street where I live, lies the spot where Walter Rathenau, then serving as foreign minister, was machine-gunned to death in his car on June 24, 1922. A gray stone memorial, erected in 1946, marks the location; this week a large wreath of flowers suddenly appeared there, placed by students and teachers from the local school named in his memory.

This volume, like this location, has a long history, and it embodies its intellectual project in several ways. I have long been concerned about the gap that divides academic Biblical Studies from the larger humanities, the more so because it was through the study of literature and intellectual history that I first became interested in the study of the Hebrew Bible and the ancient Near East. As I worked hard in graduate school to acquire the necessary philological competence, this perception of distance—"Mind the gap!"—between the fields seemed to increase rather than to narrow.

The gap remains a concern. For all the clamor about scientific illiteracy, there is an equal degree of unfamiliarity with the perspectives, insights, and changed way of reading Scripture provided by academic Biblical Studies and Near Eastern studies. This has implications for matters of public policy. In the American context, the perception of religion in public discourse, whether from the right or from the left, tends to be one that sees the Bible in quite monolithic terms, as hierarchical and dogmatic, rather than as fostering critical thought and public debate. Some of the discussion about the role of the Supreme Court in relation to the interpretation of the Constitution—whether its job is to recover the original intent of the founders or to interpret and reapply the principles laid down in it to new contexts—seems to me to mirror the kind of debates about the relationship of a prestigious or authoritative text to later authors and communities that are identified in the current volume. Placing constitutional hermeneutics in the larger historical context might usefully complicate the current dichotomy between originalism (or original intent), on the one hand, and the living Constitution approach, on the other hand, as competing theories of interpretation. For such reasons, my goal in the current study is to help open a dialogue between academic Biblical Studies and the humanities. I hope to reach a broader readership of colleagues working in comparative literature, constitutional theory, and philosophical hermeneutics, as well as colleagues closer to home in Jewish Studies, Comparative Religion, and Biblical Studies.

This goal led to a series of choices about the structure and presentation of the argument. The study moves from the general to the particular, so as to work my way into the text and the specific thematic step-by-step. Chapter 1, "Biblical Studies as the Meeting Point of the Humanities," attempts to lay out the issues, recognizing the importance of canon theory to a number of different disciplines and noting *canon* as a promising point of intersection. I painted here in broad strokes, and I allow that contemporary theory is not as monolithic as I might imply and is itself often informed by close textual work. Chapter 2 takes the argument a step further. "Rethinking the Relation between Canon and Exegesis" tries to show the ways that academic Biblical Studies, and the approach of inner-biblical exegesis might contribute to ongoing work in comparative religions, where both canon and exegesis have received renewed attention.

With Chapter 3, "The Problem of Innovation within the Formative Canon," the argument moves into the literature of the ancient Near East and ancient Israel. The goal here is to map the strategies employed by different cultures to handle the problem of legal change. Particular attention is paid to the case of ancient Israel where special constraints existed in the literary culture, given the idea of divine revelation, which then had an impact on how authors could deal with the problem of legal history. Singled out for examination is the problem of divine justice. "The Reworking of the Principle of Transgenerational Punishment," Chapter 4, examines Lamentations 5, Ezekiel 18, Deuteronomy 7, and the Targum of the Decalogue, to show various means of negotiating the problem of legal change, both in the period prior to canonization and then, for comparative purposes, in the period after the closure of the canon. Seeking to highlight the literary sophistication and technical skill of the authors, I term the cluster of strategies that they employed "a rhetoric of concealment." Although this kind of active terminology carries the risk of being easily misconstrued, the greater risk, I feel, lies in "dumbing down" the text and overlooking the thought, effort, and skill evident in how ancient authors responded to the problem of transgenerational punishment. The biblical text preserves a powerful witness to their thought and engagement.

"In my end is my beginning," as Eliot, much quoted, wrote in "Four Quartets," itself, in so many ways, a poem that would not work but for the ways that it draws upon and interacts with the canons both of Scripture and secular literature. Chapter 5, "The Canon as Sponsor of Innovation," returns to the larger project, limning the implications of this project for a more robust understanding of the canon and the nature of the hermeneutics that it embeds.

Chapter 6 marks something of a new beginning and attempts to provide an intellectual genealogy of inner-biblical exegesis, placing it in the history of the discipline of Biblical Studies. "The Phenomenon of Rewriting within the Hebrew Bible," the title of the chapter, uses the term *rewriting* to reflect the French term, *relecture*, and the German, *Fortschreibung*; both scholarly communities have made essential contributions to what North Americans call inner-biblical exegesis. Particular attention is paid in this bibliographical essay to authors whose scholarship may be less well known to many English readers, and whose major work remains available only in the German, French, or Hebrew original, or to those whose work, because of its source-critical or text-critical focus, may not at first glance be associated with this approach. The goal of this chapter is not only to make the method more accessible but also to show how integral it is to the discipline of Biblical Studies, as inner-biblical exegesis contributes new ways to understand the compositional history of the Pentateuch, the redaction of the Prophets, and the reuse of sources in the Writings.

Many whose work is discussed in Chapter 6 are those to whom I owe personal debts of gratitude. Two decades ago at Brandeis University, Michael Fishbane introduced me to inner-biblical exegesis, directed my dissertation, and, most important, encouraged my independent path. His careful work on the formula for transgenerational punishment in *Biblical Interpretation in Ancient Israel* helped inspire the reflections here. During a previous year in Germany, in 1993, I was fortunate to be able to work with both Norbert Lohfink (Frankfurt) and Eckart Otto (then Mainz, now Munich), which helped the crucial world of German biblical scholarship come alive for me. In subsequent years, additional relationships have been forged and work exchanged with Reinhard Kratz (Göttingen) and Christoph Levin (Munich). Konrad Schmid (Zürich) generously reviewed the section on Odil Hannes Steck in this volume. An e-mail exchange with Adele Berlin (College Park) several years ago pushed me to rethink some of my assumptions about Ruth. (In March 2008, just as I was reviewing page proofs for this volume, she shared with me her fine study, "Legal Fiction: Torah Law in the

Book of Ruth" [lecture for conference at Bar Ilan University, May 2008], which I regret not being able to take into account.) Anselm Hagedorn (Berlin) read an early version of the manuscript while completing his Habilitation and provided many helpful bibliographical suggestions. David Myers of UCLA provided helpful suggestions for my analysis of Simon Rawidowicz. Conversations with my departmental colleagues Jeffrey Stackert and Alex Jassen of the University of Minnesota (Minneapolis) were very helpful at a number of points. Several close colleagues in other departments provided valuable feedback, especially on the interdisciplinary dimensions of this project: John Watkins (English), Bruno Chaouat (French), and Leslie Morris (German/Jewish Studies). Subsequently, here in Berlin at the Institute for Advanced Studies, conversations with my new colleague Patricia Kitcher (New York) helped refine my discussion of Immanuel Kant.

The present volume extensively revises and expands an earlier French version, *L'Herméneutique de l'innovation: Canon et exégèse dans l'Israël biblique* (Le livre et le rouleau 24; Brussels: Éditions Lessius, 2005). The first section of that volume was a translation of my article, "'You Must Not Add Anything to What I Command You': Paradoxes of Canon and Authorship in Ancient Israel," *Numen: International Review for the History of Religions* 50 (2003): 1–51. Jean-Pierre Sonnet, the academic director of Éditions Lessius and himself a scholar of Deuteronomy and inner-biblical exegesis, first proposed that the French volume include a bibliographical essay on inner-biblical exegesis. He made valuable comments and was a constant source of encouragement. It came as a great honor when I learned that Jean Louis Ska (Rome) agreed to provide the avant-propos for that French volume. His remarks have been translated here to serve as the foreword to this volume, although they have not been adjusted to the larger format. I am indebted to Professor Ska and Éditions Lessius for this courtesy.

Literary reworking is not only the subject but also the means of *Legal Revision and Religious Renewal in Ancient Israel.* This volume is twice the length of the previous French one; significant new material has been added throughout, and a number of positions (especially in the case of Ruth) have been substantially rethought. Some colleagues' published responses to the French volume have also been taken into account. The manuscript has, accordingly, gone through many drafts. In the process, I have received welcome comments and editing help from Julie Plaut (Minneapolis/Providence). Elliot Rabin (New York) prepared the translation of the foreword and helped with editing. Hanne Løland (Oslo) provided thoughtful commentary on several sections as the manuscript drew to a close. My capable research assistants, Karen L. O'Brien (B.A., M.L.I.S.) and Michael Bartos (M.A.), maintained their sense of humor as electronic files, filled with multicolored comments and tracked changes in Word, crossed the Atlantic multiple times per day. Michael also prepared the extensive indexes for the volume. Anoop Chaturvedi, project manager at Aptara, Cambridge's typesetting group in New Delhi, set a high standard for both accuracy and customer service. It was a pleasure to work with him and his team. Finally, it was an honor to have this book approved for publication by the Syndics of

Cambridge University Press, and I would like to thank Andy Beck, as religion editor, for his encouragement, as well as the two anonymous referees for their constructive reports.

I would be happy if, in commemoration of this German holiday, this volume might help stimulate some greater reintegration between Biblical Studies and the humanities, as well as greater integration of the methods used by fellow Bible scholars.

Grunewald, Wissenschaftskolleg zu Berlin B.M.L.
October 3, 2007

Abbreviations

TEXTS AND EDITIONS

b.	*Babli*: Talmudic tractate cited in the version of the Babylonian Talmud
Ber.	*Berakot*
NJPS	*Tanakh: The Holy Scriptures. The New JPS Translation according to the Traditional Hebrew Text*
m.	*mishnah*
Mak.	*Makkot*
MT	Masoretic Text (of the OT)
NRSV	New Revised Standard Version
Sanh.	*Sanhedrin*
Šebu.	*Šebuʿot*
Tg. Onq.	*Targum Onqelos*

PERIODICALS, REFERENCE WORKS, AND SERIALS

AB	Anchor Bible
AcT	*Acta theologica*
AnBib	Analecta biblica
AS	Assyriological Studies
ATD	Das Alte Testament Deutsch
ATM	Altes Testament und Moderne
BaghMB	Baghdader Mitteilungen: Beiheft
BBB	Bonner biblische Beiträge

BEATAJ	Beiträge zur Erforschung des Alten Testaments und des antiken Judentums
BETL	Bibliotheca ephemeridum theologicarum lovaniensium
Bib	*Biblica*
BJS	Brown Judaic Studies
BN	*Biblische Notizen*
BO	*Bibliotheca orientalis*
BThSt	Biblisch-theologische Studien
BWA(N)T	Beiträge zur Wissenschaft vom Alten (und Neuen) Testament
BZ	Biblische Zeitschrift
BZAR	Beihefte zur Zeitschrift für Altorientalische und Biblische Rechtsgeschichte
BZAW	Beihefte zur Zeitschrift für die alttestamentliche Wissenschaft
CBQ	*Catholic Biblical Quarterly*
CBQMS	Catholic Biblical Quarterly Monograph Series
ConBOT	Coniectanea biblica: Old Testament Series
CRINT	Compendia rerum iudaicarum ad Novum Testamentum
CSHJ	Chicago Studies in the History of Judaism
DJD	Discoveries in the Judean Desert
DMOA	Documenta et Monumenta Orientis Antiqui
DSD	*Dead Sea Discoveries: A Journal of Current Research on the Scrolls and Related Literature*
EgT	*Église et théologie*
ErJb	*Eranos-Jahrbuch*
FAT	Forschungen zum Alten Testament
FRLANT	Forschungen zur Religion und Literatur des Alten und Neuen Testaments
Greg	*Gregorianum*
GTA	Göttinger theologischer Arbeiten
HBS	Herders biblische Studien
HSM	Harvard Semitic Monographs
HSS	Harvard Semitic Studies
HThKAT	Herders theologischer Kommentar zum Alten Testament
ICC	International Critical Commentary
JAOS	*Journal of the American Oriental Society*
JBL	*Journal of Biblical Literature*

JHS	*Journal of Hebrew Scriptures* [http://www.jhsonline.org]
JJS	*Journal of Jewish Studies*
JQR	*Jewish Quarterly Review*
JR	*Journal of Religion*
JSOT	*Journal for the Study of the Old Testament*
JSOTSup	Journal for the Study of the Old Testament Supplement Series
JSQ	*Jewish Studies Quarterly*
JSS	*Journal of Semitic Studies*
KAT	Kommentar zum Alten Testament
Maarav	*Maarav: A Journal for the Study of the Northwest Semitic Languages and Literatures*
MBPF	Münchener Beiträge zur Papyrusforschung und antiken Rechtsgeschichte
NCB	New Century Bible
NEchtB	Neue Echter Bibel
NICOT	New International Commentary on the Old Testament
Numen	*Numen: International Review for the History of Religions*
OBO	Orbis biblicus et orientalis
ÖBS	Österreichische biblische Studien
OTL	Old Testament Library
OTS	Old Testament Studies
PAAJR	*Proceedings of the American Academy of Jewish Research*
Proof	*Prooftexts: A Journal of Jewish Literary History*
QD	Quaestiones disputatae
RB	*Revue biblique*
RBL	*Review of Biblical Literature* [http://www.bookreviews.org/]
RevQ	*Revue de Qumrân*
RIDA	*Revue internationale des droits de l'antiquité*
RSR	*Recherches de science religieuse*
RTL	*Revue théologique de Louvain*
SAA	State Archives of Assyria
SBAB	Stuttgarter biblische Aufsatzbände
SBLBMI	Society of Biblical Literature The Bible and Its Modern Interpreters
SBLDS	Society of Biblical Literature Dissertation Series

SBLMS	Society of Biblical Literature Monograph Series
SBLSCS	Society of Biblical Literature Septuagint and Cognate Studies
SBLSymS	Society of Biblical Literature Symposium Series
SBLWAW	Society of Biblical Literature Writings from the Ancient World
SBS	Stuttgarter Bibelstudien
ScrHier	Scripta hierosolymitana
SHR	Studies in the History of Religions (supplement to *Numen*)
SJLA	Studies in Judaism in Late Antiquity
STDJ	Studies on the Texts of the Desert of Judah
Tarbiz	*Tarbiz: A Quarterly for Jewish Studies*
TB	Theologische Bücherei: Neudrucke und Berichte aus dem 20. Jahrhundert
Textus	*Textus: Annual of the Hebrew University Bible Project*
ThWAT	*Theologisches Wörterbuch zum Alten Testament.* Edited by G. Johannes Botterweck, Heinz-Josef Fabry, and Helmer Ringgren. 10 vols. Stuttgart: Kohlhammer, 1970–.
TLZ	*Theologische Literaturzeitung*
TRu	*Theologische Rundschau*
TZ	*Theologische Zeitschrift*
UTB	Uni-Taschenbücher
VT	*Vetus Testamentum*
VTSup	Vetus Testamentum Supplements
VWGTh	Veröffentlichungen der Wissenschaftlichen Gesellschaft für Theologie
WMANT	Wissenschaftliche Monographien zum Alten und Neuen Testament
WUNT	Wissenschaftliche Untersuchungen zum Neuen Testament
ZABR	*Zeitschrift für Altorientalische und Biblische Rechtsgeschichte*
ZAW	*Zeitschrift für die alttestamentliche Wissenschaft*
ZBKAT	Zürcher Bibelkommentare: Altes Testament
ZTK	*Zeitschrift für Theologie und Kirche*

1

Biblical Studies as the Meeting Point of the Humanities

The ideal does not always translate into the real. Just at the point where the speaker of Deuteronomy begins to propound a utopian program to eliminate poverty—"There shall be no one in need among you!" (Deut 15:4)—he quickly pulls himself back to earth to confront the gap between vision and reality: "If there is one in need among you . . . " (Deut 15:7). Utopian vision and pragmatic preparation are here separated only by a single word, since the Hebrew phrases involved are otherwise identical.[1] The

[1] Precisely that similarity of construction points to an editorial interpolation. From a historical-critical point of view, the statement in Deut 15:4 is most likely the work of a later editor, stressing the benefits that follow from obedience to the Torah, supplementing but also contradicting the original text, whereby Deut 15:7 would have been the continuation of Deut 15:3. See A. D. H. Mayes, *Deuteronomy* (NCB; London: Marshall, Morgan & Scott, 1979), 248. With the insertion marked by its close correspondence to the original text, at issue is a variation of a formal scribal technique, the repetitive resumption or *Wiederaufnahme*, as a marker of editorial activity. On this and related editorial markers, see Bernard M. Levinson, *Deuteronomy and the Hermeneutics of Legal Innovation* (New York: Oxford University Press, 1997), 17–20; and later in this volume at p. 117.

same particle that adds declamatory force to the initial assertion (כי) is also the one that forms the later conditional statement. As with the ancient text, so with contemporary scholarship: the dividing line between utopian vision and pragmatic reality hinges on a single word. In an ideal world, the concept of canon might provide a meeting point for the humanities. It would offer a bridge between the multiple, separate disciplines that operate, more or less explicitly, with canonical collections of texts and even canonical methods of research. The reality, however, is that, even as the separate disciplines actively reassess their canons—the intellectual and historical forces that defined their canons, the ideologies and biases encoded in those canons, the degree of adaptability of those canons, and the extent to which their canons promote or inhibit cultural change and intellectual renewal—there is a striking absence of dialogue between disciplines on the canon as the common point of ferment.

Even more striking than this lack of interdisciplinary dialogue is the failure of contemporary theory to engage with academic Biblical Studies.[2] A number of Bible scholars have sought to take postmodern theory into account in their work and to explore its impact upon biblical scholarship.[3] It seems to me that colleagues in comparative

[2] As noted by Jonathan Z. Smith, "Canons, Catalogues and Classics," in *Canonization and Decanonization: Papers Presented to the International Conference of the Leiden Institute for the Study of Religions (LISOR), Held at Leiden, 9–10 January 1997* (ed. Arie van der Kooij and Karel van der Toorn; SHR 82; Leiden: E. J. Brill, 1998), 295–311 (at 295–96).

[3] John J. Collins, *The Bible after Babel: Historical Criticism in a Postmodern Age* (Grand Rapids, Mich.: William B. Eerdmans, 2005); and, using empire theory and postcolonial theory to help explain the

literature and related fields have not engaged historical-critical work in Biblical Studies to the same degree.[4] The contemporary turn away from philology, as if it were not a humanistic discipline, contributes to this problem.[5] Even the recent infatuation of some literary theorists with ancient Jewish midrash is no exception. It romanticizes rabbinic hermeneutics as championing radical textual indeterminacy, and thus heralds the ancient rabbis as the precursors of modern critical trends.[6] By

promulgation of the Pentateuch, Anselm C. Hagedorn, "Local Law in an Imperial Context: The Role of Torah in the (Imagined) Persian Period," in *The Pentateuch as Torah: New Models for Understanding Its Promulgation and Acceptance* (ed. Gary N. Knoppers and Bernard M. Levinson; Winona Lake, Ind.: Eisenbrauns, 2007), 57–76. See further Robert P. Carroll, "Poststructuralist Approaches: New Historicism and Postmodernism," in *The Cambridge Companion to Biblical Interpretation* (ed. John Barton; Cambridge: Cambridge University Press), 50–66; Keith Whitelam, *The Invention of Ancient Israel: The Silencing of Palestinian History* (London: Routledge, 1997); George Aichele et al. [as the Bible and Culture Collective], *The Postmodern Bible* (New Haven, Conn.: Yale University Press, 1995).

4 Several literary scholars have made serious such attempts, the most intense effort being that of Meir Sternberg, *Hebrews between Cultures: Group Portraits and National Literature* (Bloomington: Indiana University Press, 1998; and that of James Nohrnberg, *Like unto Moses: The Constitution of an Interruption* (Bloomington: Indiana University Press, 1995). On Sternberg's isolation from the current state of Biblical Studies, see the reviews by Francis Landy, *JHS* 3 (2000–2001), http://www.arts.ualberta.ca/JHS/reviews/review013.htm; cited September 28, 2007; and Stephen P. Weitzman, *JQR* 94 (2004): 537–41.

5 See the passionate affirmation of and nostalgia for philology in the posthumously published volume by Edward W. Said, *Humanism and Democratic Criticism* (Columbia Themes in Philosophy; New York: Columbia University Press, 2004). Especially significant are the essays "The Return to Philology" and "Introduction to Erich Auerbach's *Mimesis*" (57–84 and 85–118).

6 See *Midrash and Literature* (ed. Geoffrey H. Hartman and Sanford Budick; New Haven, Conn.: Yale University Press, 1986).

disregarding the importance of law and privileging narrative, that approach completely distorts the priorities of classical rabbinic interpretation, and thus amounts to a projection onto the sources rather than a critical engagement with them.[7] As in psychoanalysis, so also in literary history: a projection always involves a repression, one that seems to apply more broadly in this case. At the precise moment when the canon has become such a point of contention in the humanities, critically absent from the discussion is academic Biblical Studies: the one discipline devoted to exploring what a canon is, how it emerges historically, how its texts relate to one another, and how it affects the community that espouses it.[8]

The same omission in comparative research on Scripture by academic Religious Studies, the sister discipline of Biblical Studies, only doubles the irony. That omission is

[7] In support of the position argued here, see Daniel Boyarin, *Intertextuality and the Reading of Midrash* (Bloomington: Indiana University Press, 1990), 35–38; David Stern, "Literary Criticism or Literary Homilies? Susan Handelman and the Contemporary Study of Midrash," *Proof* 5 (1985): 96–103; idem, "Midrash and Hermeneutics: Polysemy vs. Indeterminacy," in idem, *Midrash and Theory: Ancient Jewish Exegesis and Contemporary Literary Studies* (Evanston, Ill.: Northwestern University Press, 1996), 15–38; and Azzan Yadin, "The Hammer on the Rock: Mekhilta Deuteronomy and the Question of Rabbinic Polysemy," *JSQ* 9 (2002): 1–27.

[8] One might profitably consult *One Scripture or Many? Canon from Biblical, Theological and Philosophical Perspectives* (ed. Christine Helmer and Christof Landmesser; Oxford: Oxford University Press, 2004). In contrast, in an otherwise stimulating exploration of the significance of canon for law and constitutional theory, scripture is only invoked once, in a pro forma etymology of the word (J. M. Balkin and Sanford Levinson, *Legal Canons* [New York: New York University Press, 2000], 32n1). Neither the editors nor the contributors explore whether Biblical Studies might provide a useful model for understanding legal hermeneutics.

evident, for example, in the otherwise valuable collection, *Rethinking Scripture: Essays from a Comparative Perspective*.[9] Despite the stated goal of rethinking older models, the volume inadvertently reifies older assumptions by using the completed canon of Scripture as its intellectual point of departure. The absence of a contribution by a biblical scholar ironically perpetuates the gap between the comparative study of religion and philological analysis of the scriptural sources of religion. Barbara A. Holdrege may well be justified in pointing out that "biblical and orientalist scholars . . . have focused on particular religious texts rather than on scripture as a general religious phenomenon."[10] Nonetheless, the opposite extreme also entails a risk. It makes her essay's stated goal—to recover the immanent religiosity associated with texts in ancient Israel—methodologically impossible to achieve. Holdrege construes the ancient Israelite sources from the perspective of how they are read by later Jewish tradition, not how they functioned and were read in ancient Israel itself. This anachronistic frame of reference is evident as she describes the biblical Hymn to Wisdom (Prov 8:22–31) as a "pre-Rabbinic text."[11]

This absence of dialogue with Biblical Studies impoverishes contemporary theory in disciplines across the humanities and deprives it of intellectual models that

[9] See *Rethinking Scripture: Essays from a Comparative Perspective* (ed. Miriam Levering; Albany: State University of New York Press, 1989).

[10] Barbara A. Holdrege, "The Bride of Israel: The Ontological Status of Scripture in the Rabbinic and Kabbalistic Traditions," in *Rethinking Scripture*, 180–261 (at 180).

[11] Holdrege, "Bride of Israel," 188. See also eadem, *Veda and Torah: Transcending the Textuality of Scripture* (Albany: State University of New York Press, 1996).

would actually advance its own project. Making this argument from a different perspective, Robert Alter rejects the postmodern view of the canon as a form of "ideological coercion" and argues instead that it points to a "transhistorical textual community."[12] But while my sympathies lie with that alternative approach, my historical training makes me apply a hermeneutics of suspicion to it. The very concept of transhistorical textual community is itself a construction, or perhaps a counter-construction, that affirms certain values. It is not clear to me that the earliest anthologies of authoritative or prestigious texts for Second Temple Judaism were assembled for purely "transhistorical" purposes. More likely, such collections would have been intended to provide a bulwark against Greco-Roman culture or even against dominant forms of Second Temple Judaism, as in the case of the Samarian/Samaritan community with its Pentateuch or the community at Wadi Qumran, with the Dead Sea Scrolls. From this perspective, any transhistorical community that comes into existence through the canon is already a transformation of some earlier community served by the canon. Surely the Dutch Reformed Church's appropriation of the canon through most of the past century to legitimate apartheid in South Africa was not a disinterested enterprise, any more than the important ways that the Bible is currently being used

[12] Robert Alter, *Canon and Creativity: Modern Writing and the Authority of Scripture* (New Haven, Conn.: Yale University Press, 2000), 5. In contrast, Frank Kermode's recent advocacy of the canon is, uncharacteristically, intellectually tepid. It works with a vague notion of aesthetic pleasure that does not clearly engage ethical issues or the social location of a canon. See idem, *Pleasure and Change: The Aesthetics of Canon* (ed. Robert Alter; The Berkeley Tanner Lectures; New York: Oxford University Press, 2004).

in South Africa to help renew a postapartheid society, now based upon equality.[13]

German Studies provides an example of how the comparative perspective of the biblical canon might offer a richer perspective on ostensibly discipline-specific questions. The more the discipline investigates its own history, the more salient is the missing dialogue with Biblical Studies. There was no German nation-state until the unification of the scores of German-speaking kingdoms, principalities, and free towns by Otto von Bismarck in 1871. But German writers and thinkers of the eighteenth and nineteenth centuries had already laid its groundwork through their promulgation of a common art, literature, and music that united German speakers as a *Kulturnation.*

Although not yet an independent political entity, the German nation already existed as a *Land der Dichter und Denker* [land of poets and thinkers].[14] The German nation

[13] See Louis Jonker, "Reforming History: The Hermeneutical Significance of the Books of Chronicles," *VT* 57 (2007): 21–44.

[14] Germanists often attribute this phrase to the French writer and traveler Madame de Staël (1766–1817), in her influential, *De l'Allemagne* (1810), although it never appears in her work. At best, she refers to Germany as "la patrie de la pensée"; elsewhere, she notes "La plupart *des écrivains et des penseurs* travaillent dans la solitude . . . " (Mme La Baronne [Anne-Louise-Germaine] de Staël Holstein, *De l'Allemagne* [3 vols.; Paris: H. Nicolle, 1810; reprint, London: John Murray, 1813], 1: 5, 16 [emphasis added]; eadem, *De l'Allemagne: Nouvelle Édition* [ed. Jean de Pange and Simone Balayé; 5 vols.; Paris: Hachette, 1958], 1: 21, 38). The attribution to de Staël is repeatedly assumed, however, by the highly regarded philosopher and essayist Helmuth Plessner, where *diese Lobesformel* [formula of praise] is rapidly inverted into an alliterative lament for what was lost. See Helmuth Plessner, "Ein Volk der Dichter und Denker?: Zu einem Wort der Madame de Staël" [1964], in *Gesammelte Schriften*, vol. 6: *Die verspätete Nation* (ed. Günter Dux et al.; Frankfurt: Suhrkamp,

was in effect created and sustained by its literary canon before it had a unified political existence. That situation cries out for an exploration of the parallel with how the scriptural canon sustained "the People of the Book" for the two millennia of their life in the Diaspora. Heinrich Heine's much-touted notion of the Bible as "ein portatives Vaterland" [a portable Fatherland], more frequently invoked than critically examined, does not seem very helpful in this context.[15] However conveniently it has become a facile catchword for recent work in diaspora poetics and

---

1982), 281–91. The cliché is widespread on the Internet, even on university Web sites (http://www.uni-rostock.de/fakult/philfak/fkw/iph/thies/19.Jahrhundert.html) and official sources of information, such as the state library of Rheinland-Pfalz (http://www.lbz-rlp.de/cms/landesbibliothekszentrum/presse/pressemeldungen/pressemeldung/artikel/71/46/index.html?no_cache=1&tx_ttnews%5BpS%5D=1175613624&cHash=a3f93f6e6b) (cited April 10, 2007). On the phrase as a comforting panacea at odds with twentieth-century history, see Jeffrey L. Sammons, "The Land Where the Canon B(l)ooms: Observations on the German Canon and Its Opponents, There and Here," in *Canon vs. Culture: Reflections on the Current Debate* (Wellesley Studies in Critical Theory, Literary History, and Culture 23; New York: Garland, 2001), 117–33 (at 119). On the German reception of de Staël's work, see Michel Espagne, "'De l'Allemagne,'" in *Deutsche Erinnerungsorte* (ed. Etienne François and Hagen Schulze; 3 vols.; 4th ed.; Munich: C. H. Beck, 2002), 1: 225–41.

15 For Heinrich Heine's original quote, see idem, *Geständnisse: Geschrieben im Winter 1854*; reprinted in Heinrich Heine, *Sämtliche Schriften in zwölf Bänden*, vol. 11: *Schriften 1851–1855* (ed. Klaus Briegleb; Munich: Hanser Verlag, 1968), 483. Within biblical studies, Frank Crüsemann has directed new attention to the quote in his essay on the function and development of the canon of the Old Testament ("'Das portative Vaterland': Struktur und Genese des alttestamentlichen Kanons," in idem, *Kanon und Sozialgeschichte: Beiträge zum Alten Testament* (Gütersloh: Chr. Kaiser/Gütersloher Verlagshaus, 2003), 227–49. However, he does not investigate how the quote functions for Heine, and assumes the accuracy of the

Old Testament theology, Heine's metaphor does not offer an informed reading of Jewish literary or social history.[16] It has much more to do with Heine's own well-justified sense of dislocation and rejection—and thus with yearning for membership in a German literary tradition from which he was excluded. Despite his eager attempts to find acceptance as a German writer, even after baptism, he continued to be regarded by Germans as a Jew. Thereafter, he emigrated to France, where, in irony that seems bitterly inevitable, he was considered a German exile.[17]

The extent to which the classical past of the German literary canon is actually an ideological construction, an ex post facto product of deliberate shaping by later "editors" of that canon, only reinforces the relevance of the missing perspective of Biblical Studies, where such issues have long been recognized in the shaping of the canon. Using a range of techniques already well honed by their ancient religious counterparts, therefore, German literary historians of the nineteenth century modified medieval manuscripts before publication, excised early "Frenchified" novels from their studies, and sanctified works by Goethe and Schiller as

quote as a description for how Jewish identity was maintained in the Diaspora.

16 In medieval Judaism, for example, Scripture is not metaphorically described in terms of homeland, nor did it replace Zion in its symbolic power. More accurately, the community would achieve its continuity and grounding in terms of ritual, halakic observance, and community organization. If anything, the shared longing for a homeland would provide a means for cultural identity and self-definition. Scripture itself would have played a secondary or tertiary role.

17 See Anat Feinberg, "Abiding in a Haunted House: The Issue of *Heimat* in Contemporary German-Jewish Writing," *New German Critique* 70 (1997): 161–81.

classic, all in order to recover a "true" German character unsullied by any influences too foreign, modern, or feminine.[18] Early-modern German editors may have differed significantly in ideology from their ancient Near Eastern counterparts, but they employed strikingly similar techniques (literary and linguistic selectivity) to pursue a common goal: the creation of a pristine past that can serve as an enduring charter. The same issue of ideological shaping has also been identified in recent work on the "construction" of the disciplines of Theology, Classics, and Oriental Studies in German universities during the nineteenth century.[19]

In addition to intellectual models, there is something more fundamental at stake. Biblical Studies provides a way of critically engaging the ideological assumptions of contemporary theory, whose objections to the notion of a canon are certainly understandable: for being exclusive; for encoding class, race, or gender bias; for silencing competing or less prestigious voices; for ignoring difference; for arresting social change; for enshrining privilege. Yet in

[18] For the discipline's struggles with this legacy, see *Rethinking "Germanistik": Canon and Culture* (ed. Robert Bledsoe et al.; Berkeley Insights in Linguistics and Semiotics 6; New York: Peter Lang, 1991).

[19] See Susannah Heschel, *Abraham Geiger and the Jewish Jesus* (CSHJ; Chicago: University of Chicago Press, 1998); Thomas Albert Howard, *Religion and the Rise of Historicism: W. M. L. de Wette, Jacob Burckhardt, and the Theological Origins of Nineteenth-Century Historical Consciousness* (Cambridge: Cambridge University Press, 2000); idem, *Protestant Theology and the Making of the Modern German University* (New York: Oxford University Press, 2006); Suzanne L. Marchand, "Philhellenism and the *Furor Orientalis,*" *Modern Intellectual History* 1 (2004): 331–58; and Christian Wiese, *Challenging Colonial Discourse: Jewish Studies and Protestant Theology in Wilhelmine Germany* (trans. Barbara Harshav; Studies in Jewish History and Culture 10; Leiden: E. J. Brill, 2005).

all such cases, the canon is taken to be a self-sufficient, unchanging entity, one that not only properly demands deconstruction but also outright rejection. But, in being read that way, the deconstruction of the canon itself entails an alternative construction, ahistorically conceptualizing the canon from the perspective of the present, whereby it appears closed, both literally and metaphorically. Too often, that approach remains blind to its own lack of historical ground. It locates critique as something external to the canon, thus transforming the canon into a lifeless literary fossil. The contrary premise here is that critical theory is not at odds with the canon but central to the canon and sanctioned by it.[20] From that point of view, Biblical Studies must submit itself to this self-same process of examining its own theoretical constructs and methodological assumptions. There is no priority of completed, authoritative canon to human critical engagement with the canon, either chronologically or ontologically. Properly understood, the canon is radically open: it models critique and embeds theory. By recovering that absent perspective, this short work seeks to open the conversation between Biblical Studies and the humanities.

[20] See Herbert N. Schneidau, *Sacred Discontent: The Bible and Western Tradition* (Berkeley: University of California Press, 1977); Brayton Polka, *The Dialectic of Biblical Critique: Interpretation and Existence* (New York: St. Martin's, 1986); and idem, *Truth and Interpretation: An Essay in Thinking* (New York: St. Martin's; London: Macmillan, 1990).

2

Rethinking the Relation between "Canon" and "Exegesis"

The idea of a scriptural canon is one of the most distinctive achievements of many major religions, both Western (Zoroastrianism, Judaism, Christianity, and Islām) and Eastern (the Pāli canon of Theravāda Buddhism).[1] By locating its font of revelation or contemplative insight in foundational sources, however, a culture confronts an almost inevitable difficulty. The essence of a canon is that it be stable, self-sufficient, and delimited. As Moses twice admonished his addressees in Deuteronomy: "You must not add anything to what I command you nor take anything away from it, but shall keep the commandments of Yahweh your God" (Deut 4:2; similarly 13:1 [English, 12:32]).[2] In the Bible, this so-called canon formula occurs

[1] For a valuable comparative perspective, see *Canonization and Decanonization: Papers Presented to the International Conference of the Leiden Institute for the Study of Religions (LISOR), Held at Leiden, 9–10 January 1997* (ed. Arie van der Kooij and Karel van der Toorn; SHR 82; Leiden: E. J. Brill, 1998).

[2] See Bernard M. Levinson, "The Neo-Assyrian Origins of the Canon Formula in Deuteronomy 13:1," in *Scriptural Exegesis: The Shapes of Culture and the Religious Imagination (Essays in Honour of Michael*

primarily in the context of Israelite wisdom literature (Qoh 3:14; 12:12–13; cf. Sir 42:21; Rev 22:18–19). The association with any notion of canon, however, marks a postbiblical development. The formula actually has a long prehistory in the ancient Near East, where it originally sought to prevent royal inscriptions, including law collections and treaties (cf. 1 Macc 8:30), from being altered. In other contexts, it affirmed the adequacy of wisdom instruction.[3] Only subsequently was it taken over by Deuteronomy's Israelite authors and applied to the Mosaic Torah.[4] The

---

Fishbane) (ed. Deborah A. Green and Laura S. Lieber; Oxford: Oxford University Press, forthcoming in 2009).

3 Adducing comparative material, see Johannes Leipoldt and Siegfried Morenz, *Heilige Schriften: Betrachtungen zur Religionsgeschichte der antiken Mittelmeerwelt* (Leipzig: Harrassowitz, 1953), 53–65 (stressing the origins of the formula in Egyptian wisdom literature); Nahum M. Sarna, "Psalm 89: A Study in Inner Biblical Exegesis," in *Biblical and Other Studies* (ed. Alexander Altmann; Brandeis University Studies and Texts 1; Cambridge, Mass.: Harvard University Press, 1963), 29–46, reprinted in idem, *Studies in Biblical Interpretation* (JPS Scholar of Distinction Series; Philadelphia: Jewish Publication Society, 2000), 377–94 (stressing precedents in cuneiform literature); Moshe Weinfeld, *Deuteronomy and the Deuteronomic School* (Oxford: Clarendon, 1972; reprint, Winona Lake, Ind.: Eisenbrauns, 1992), 261–65 (with a wide range of Near Eastern and Egyptian parallels); Michael Fishbane, "Varia Deuteronomica," *ZAW* 84 (1972): 349–52; Eleonore Reuter, "'Nimm nichts davon weg und füge nichts hinzu': Dtn 13,1, seine alttestamentlichen Parallelen und seine altorientalischen Vorbilder," *BN* 47 (1989): 107–14; Christoph Dohmen and Manfred Oeming, *Biblischer Kanon: Warum und Wozu? Eine Kanontheologie* (QD 137; Freiburg: Herder, 1992), 68–89; and Choon-Leong Seow, *Ecclesiastes* (AB 18C; New York: Doubleday, 1997), 388, 394 (stressing that the formula's original intent was not to delimit a corpus of texts as canonical but to emphasize "the sufficiency of the text").

4 For similar phenomena in the world of archaic and classical Greece, see Karl-Joachim Hölkeskamp, *Schiedsrichter, Gesetzgeber und Gesetzgebung im archaischen Griechenland* (Historia-Einzelschrift 131; Stuttgart: Franz Steiner, 1999); idem, "(In)Schrift und

formula makes it clear that its intent is to preclude both literary and doctrinal innovation by safeguarding the textual status quo.

With such fixity and textual sufficiency as its hallmarks, how can a canon be made to address the varying needs of later generations of religious communities? These later generations face the conflicting imperatives of subsuming their lives to the authority of the canon while adapting that unchangeable canon to realities of social, economic, political, and intellectual life never contemplated at the time of its composition. Among the vicissitudes not contemplated by the canons foundational to the three major Western monotheisms are, for example, for Judaism, the Roman destruction of the Jerusalem Temple in 70 C.E. that rendered impossible the sacrificial cultus essential to Israelite religion; for Christianity, a Messiah who failed to return, although that return in eschatological Parousia had been expected to be imminent; and, for Islām, the death of Muḥammad, the community's founder and prophetic leader, without his having appointed a successor. Of course, the theology of *O felix culpa* extends to the History of Religions, where crisis may engender a productive innovation. The triumph of Pharisaic Judaism as the dominant form of Judaism, with the claim that its teachings derive by oral transmission from Sinaitic revelation; the consolidation of the church in doctrine, organization,

---

Monument: Zum Begriff des Gesetzes im archaischen und klassischen Griechenland," *Zeitschrift für Papyrologie und Epigraphik* 132 (2000): 73–96 (at 84–87); and Anselm C. Hagedorn, *Between Moses and Plato: Individual and Society in Deuteronomy and Ancient Greek Law* (FRLANT 204; Göttingen: Vandenhoeck & Ruprecht, 2004), 76–78, 163.

and admission of Gentiles; and the separate developments of Sunni and Shiʿi Islām are in many ways the results of just those cases where the scriptural canon faced historical circumstances that threatened its viability.

If the closed literary canon as the repository of revelation or insight is the source of stability for a religious tradition, exegesis provides vitality. By *exegesis* or *hermeneutics* I mean the range of interpretive strategies designed to extend the application of a given canon to the whole of life, even to circumstances not originally contemplated by the canon itself. By means of exegesis, the textually finite canon becomes infinite in its application. One of the chief means, therefore, by which a religious tradition demonstrates its creativity is the variety of ways it finds to accommodate itself to and overcome an authoritative yet textually delimited canon.[5] Jonathan Z. Smith has argued that the dialectical interplay between canonical delimitation and exegetical expansion should be made central to the study of the

[5] Canonical criticism in Biblical Studies has valuably emphasized the importance of the formative canon to Israelite religion as a repository of the nation's identity. In this understanding, subsequent generations could draw on the canon and apply it to new historical crises. Despite this proper emphasis, however, the approach tends to overlook the hermeneutical problematic inherent in just that reinterpretation and reapplication of the canon. It overlooks also the extent to which the reformulated texts challenge the authority and break down the coherence of the original texts. I therefore have some reservations about the approach of James A. Sanders, "'Adaptable for Life': The Nature and Function of Canon," in *Magnalia Dei: The Mighty Acts of God. Essays on the Bible and Archaeology in Memory of G. Ernest Wright* (ed. Frank Moore Cross, Werner E. Lemke, and Patrick D. Miller Jr.; Garden City, N.Y.: Doubleday & Co., 1976), 531–60; reprinted with a foreword in James A. Sanders, *From Sacred Story to Sacred Text: Canon as Paradigm* (Philadelphia: Fortress, 1987), 9–39.

History of Religions. He stresses that what he felicitously terms "exegetical ingenuity" represents "that most characteristic, persistent and obsessive religious activity."[6] That interplay—*conflict* might be the better word—between canonical constraint and exegetical ingenuity also took place within ancient Israel. But it is necessary to go beyond Smith's model in two key ways in order to see how.

First, the creativity of exegesis consists not only in its ability to adjust to new circumstances not contemplated by the canon but also in the interpreter's claim that there is no innovative or transformative activity involved whatsoever: the interpreter merely elucidates the plenitude of truth already latent in the canon. For example, Deuteronomy's previously mentioned canon formula already embodies just this paradoxical structure. The appeal for fidelity to the legal status quo (Deut 13:1) immediately follows a passage in which the authors have radically transformed prior religious law by demanding the restriction of all sacrifice to the central sanctuary (Deut 12). The canon formula's use in that context, in effect functioning as a colophon to Deuteronomy's radically innovative law of centralization, is therefore paradoxical.[7] This paradox in many ways marks a constant in Jewish literary and intellectual history.

[6] See Jonathan Z. Smith, "Sacred Persistence: Toward a Redescription of Canon," in idem, *Imagining Religion: From Babylon to Jonestown* (CSHJ; Chicago: University of Chicago Press, 1982), 36–52 (at 48). See Smith's further reflections on that study in idem, "Canons, Catalogues and Classics," in *Canonization and Decanonization*, 303–9.

[7] See Michael Fishbane, *Biblical Interpretation in Ancient Israel* (2d ed.; Oxford: Clarendon, 1988), 79, 263; Bernard M. Levinson, *Deuteronomy and the Hermeneutics of Legal Innovation* (New York: Oxford University Press, 1997), 17–20; and idem, "Neo-Assyrian Origins of the Canon Formula."

Gershom Scholem has shown how each successive transformation of tradition presents itself as implicit in and consistent with, rather than as a departure from, the original canon.[8] The rabbis themselves seem to have recognized the burden that they placed upon Sinai when they spoke of the Mishnah's elaborately codified system of Sabbath laws as a mountain suspended by a slim scriptural thread.[9] Although it is a profound instrument of cultural renewal, exegesis is often also profoundly a study in the false consciousness of the interpreter, who disclaims the very historical agency that, for Smith, makes exegesis worthy of study!

The second problem with Smith's model is its presupposition that exegetical ingenuity takes place subsequent to the formation of a closed canon.[10] By implication, the canon is subject to hermeneutical reapplication only after its closure; alternatively, the canon is a hermeneutical problem only postcanonically. Such a seemingly self-evident presupposition leaves unexamined the hermeneutical dynamics that operate within a culture prior to the closure of a literary canon. Thus, for example, Haim H. Cohn's analysis of the ingenious ploys used in rabbinic exegesis to transform biblical law, while seeming nonetheless to honor its authoritative status, restricts the operation of such ingenuity to the postbiblical stage while overlooking the operation of similar stratagems within biblical law

[8] See Gershom Scholem, "Revelation and Tradition as Religious Categories in Judaism," in idem, *The Messianic Idea in Judaism and Other Essays on Jewish Spirituality* (New York: Schocken, 1971), 282–303.

[9] "The laws of the Sabbath . . . are like mountains hanging by a hair, for they consist of little Bible and many laws" (*m. Ḥagigah* 1:8).

[10] Smith, "Sacred Persistence," 48.

itself.[11] It is essential to understand that the ingenuity of the interpreter operates even in the formative period of the canon, while those texts that will subsequently win authoritative status are still being composed and collected. The stakes here are important, because Smith's model in effect posits a hierarchy between canon and interpretation. That hierarchy is untenable. Interpretation is constitutive of the canon; it is not secondary to the canon in terms of either chronology or significance.[12]

[11] See Haim H. Cohn, "Legal Change in Unchangeable Law: The Talmudical Pattern," in *Legal Change: Essays in Honour of Julius Stone* (ed. A. R. Blackshield; Sydney: Butterworths, 1983), 10–33.

[12] An example of this false hierarchy in New Testament scholarship can be found in Richard E. Palmer's *Hermeneutics: Interpretation Theory in Schleiermacher, Dilthey, Heidegger, and Gadamer* (Northwestern University Studies in Phenomenology and Existential Philosophy; Evanston, Ill.: Northwestern University Press, 1969), 23–24. When Palmer reflects on the scene where the resurrected Jesus derives the necessity of a suffering Messiah from "Moses and the Prophets" (Luke 24:25–27), he takes at face value the statement by the Lukan narrator that Jesus "interpreted" the Hebrew Bible. Palmer uses the scene as a paradigm for the work of the modern reader, who must revivify the otherwise-inert ancient text. In reading the text literally, however, Palmer fails to see that the Gospel text is itself already a sophisticated product of hermeneutics. The author of Luke here provides a narrative apologia both for the concept of a Messiah who suffers and for the Christological reading of the Hebrew Bible as an Old Testament. The Lukan author thus reads hermeneutical constructions of Jesus by the later church back into Jesus as the protagonist of the Gospel narrative. Modern hermeneutical theory is here inadequate to the theory already implicit in the ancient text. Werner G. Jeanrond still views both interpretation and reception as theological categories separate from and subsequent to the composition of the text (*Text and Interpretation as Categories of Theological Thinking* [New York: Crossroad, 1988]). Contrast the strong conception of hermeneutics provided by Brayton Polka, *Truth and Interpretation: An Essay in Thinking* (New York: St. Martin's; London: Macmillan, 1990).

That much is implicitly clear thanks to the contributions of the "inner-biblical exegesis" approach to Biblical Studies over the past two decades, which has become associated in particular with Michael Fishbane and James L. Kugel.[13] This approach has contributed an important new perspective to the discipline by emphasizing the textuality of Scripture; by demonstrating the role of texts in the culture of ancient Israel and the Second Temple period; and by recognizing how ancient writers sought to explain, respond to, and challenge older texts that had already won cultural prestige.

At the same time, both scholars leave critical questions unexplored. Fishbane shows the close ties of Israelite literature to the scribal and intellectual traditions of the ancient Near East, demonstrating its sophistication and thereby also contextualizing some of the techniques employed in later rabbinic exegesis. Yet it sometimes remains unclear how the approach relates to conventional models in Biblical Studies or what criteria control the direction of literary influence claimed between texts. Kugel pointed out this

[13] See Fishbane, *Biblical Interpretation*; James L. Kugel, "Early Interpretation: The Common Background of Late Forms of Biblical Exegesis," in *Early Biblical Interpretation* (ed. James L. Kugel and Rowan Greer; Philadelphia: Westminster, 1986), 9–106; and idem, *Traditions of the Bible: A Guide to the Bible As It Was at the Start of the Common Era* (Cambridge, Mass.: Harvard University Press, 1998). Helping pioneer this approach were, among others, Sarna, "Psalm 89: A Study in Inner Biblical Exegesis"; and Jacob Weingreen, *From Bible to Mishna: The Continuity of Tradition* (Manchester: Manchester University Press, 1976). As evidence of the diffusion of this approach, see Yair Zakovitch, *An Introduction to Inner-Biblical Interpretation* (Even Yehudah: Rekhes, 1992) (Hebrew); and Eckart Otto, "Innerbiblische Exegese im Heiligkeitsgesetz Levitikus 17–26," in *Levitikus als Buch* (ed. Heinz-Josef Fabry and Hans-Winfried Jüngling; BBB 119; Berlin: Philo, 1999), 125–96.

problem in a thoughtful review. His own work brilliantly shows how a wide range of Second Temple and classical rabbinic, church, and Islamic literature responds to ambiguities, redundancies, or inconsistencies in the biblical text and seeks to resolve or embellish them. Inexplicably, however, this hermeneutical model is applied only to postbiblical literature in relation to the Bible as an already-formed, complete, authoritative, canonical text. Whether the same model might supplement the standard Documentary Hypothesis and prove useful for understanding the classical literary history of ancient Israel, including the formation of the Pentateuch, is not explored.[14]

So far, the implications of the study of inner-biblical exegesis for a broader theory of canon have not been probed. Part of the difficulty has to do with academic specialization itself, so that those concerned with broader issues of cultural meaning and theory are often not in dialogue with those whose focus is philological rigor. This essay attempts to encourage such dialogue, and to show the productivity of this approach for theoretical work in other disciplines. I therefore argue the following theses: (1) exegesis provides a strategy for religious renewal; (2) renewal and innovation

[14] James L. Kugel, "The Bible's Earliest Interpreters," *Proof* 7 (1987): 269–83. The situation that results ironically brings to mind the intellectual safeguards that nineteenth-century *Wissenschaft des Judentums* [Science of Judaism] imposed upon itself. For example, Heinrich Graetz (1817–1891) freely applied both higher and lower criticism to the Prophets and Hagiographa. "Nevertheless, he refused to apply the same to the Pentateuch, and he insisted on the unity and pre-exilic origins of the entire Torah." See Nahum M. Sarna, "Abraham Geiger and Biblical Scholarship," in idem, *Studies in Biblical Interpretation* (JPS Scholar of Distinction Series; Philadelphia: Jewish Publication Society, 2000), 161–72 (at 163).

are almost always covert rather than explicit in ancient Israel; (3) in many cases exegesis involves not the passive explication but the radical subversion of prior authoritative texts; and (4) these phenomena are found in the literature of ancient Israel before the closure of the canon.

3

The Problem of Innovation within the Formative Canon

The concept of divine revelation of law distinguishes Israelite religion from all of the other religions of the ancient Near East. According to this concept, Yahweh publicly reveals his will to Israel in the form of cultic, civil, and ethical law, obedience to which becomes the condition for the nation's proper relationship to God and possession of the promised land of Canaan. The most dramatic account of this legal revelation occurs when God, from the top of Mount Sinai, proclaims the Ten Commandments to the nation of Israel gathered at the base of the mountain, trembling in fear of the thunderous divine voice (Exod 19–20). But it is not the Ten Commandments alone that the Hebrew Bible ascribes to divine revelation. By means of a redactional tour de force, the entire legal corpus of the Pentateuch, in effect all biblical law, is either attributed directly to God or indirectly to him through Moses, his prophetic intermediary.[1]

[1] Ezekiel's vision of the restored Jerusalem and its temple (Ezek 40–48) represents a variation of this paradigm. God continues to reveal

THE LEGACY OF CUNEIFORM LAW

Despite the claim by Israelite authors for the divine origin of the legal collections, the archaeological remains of the ancient Near East preclude any notion of *lex ex nihilo*. The Near East bequeathed to ancient Israel a prestigious literary genre, the legal collection, that originated in the scribal schools (the e d u b a) of late-third-millennium Sumer and then spread up the Fertile Crescent through Babylon and Assyria into Anatolia and the Hittite Empire.[2] Since the discovery of the justly famous Laws of Hammurabi in 1901, about a dozen different cuneiform legal collections have been discovered, written in Sumerian, Akkadian, and Hittite, and ranging from school exercises to extended, formal compositions. Notwithstanding the ostensible legal

law through the mediation of a prophet: the corpus of law that is to govern the community after its return from exile here derives its authority from a new prophetic revelation.

[2] On the e d u b a (É.DUB.BA.A) or *bīt ṭuppi*, lit., "tablet house"), see Åke W. Sjöberg, "The Old Babylonian Eduba," in *Sumerological Studies in Honor of Thorkild Jacobsen on His Seventieth Birthday, June 7, 1974* (ed. Stephen J. Lieberman; AS 20; Chicago: University of Chicago Press, 1975), 159–79; Herman L. J. Vanstiphout, "On the Old Babylonian Eduba Curriculum," in *Centres of Learning: Learning and Location in Pre-Modern Europe and the Near East* (ed. Jan Willem Drijvers and Alasdair A. MacDonald; Brill's Studies in Intellectual History 61; Leiden: E. J. Brill, 1995), 3–16; Andrew R. George, "In Search of the é.dub.ba.a: The Ancient Mesopotamian School in Literature and Reality," in *"An Experienced Scribe Who Neglects Nothing": Ancient Near Eastern Studies in Honor of Jacob Klein* (ed. Yitzhak [Yitschak] Sefati et al.; Bethesda, Md.: CDL Press, 2005), 127–37; and Niek Veldhuis, *Religion, Literature, and Scholarship: The Sumerian Composition "Nanše and the Birds," with a Catalogue of Sumerian Bird Names* (Cuneiform Monographs 22; Leiden: E. J. Brill/Styx, 2004).

form, these texts were much closer to literature or philosophy than to actual law in the modern sense.[3] This status suggests itself for the following reasons. On the one hand, as a text, the Laws of Hammurabi won such cultural prestige that it was recopied for more than a millennium after its composition in roughly 1755 B.C.E., and the Neo-Assyrian King Assurbanipal included the text in his library of cultural classics at Nineveh (ca. 660 B.C.E.).[4] On the other hand, there is no evidence for the text's stipulations ever having been implemented as actual law, let alone for its being cited as prescriptive, in any of the hundreds of thousands of actual court dockets that survive from the Old Babylonian period. Its requirements seem to have had

3 On the academic nature of the legal collection, see Benno Landsberger, *The Conceptual Autonomy of the Babylonian World* (trans. Thorkild Jacobsen, Benjamin R. Foster, and Heinrich von Siebenthal; Monographs on the Ancient Near East 1/4; Malibu, Calif.: Undena, 1976); originally published as "Die Eigenbegrifflichkeit der babylonischen Welt," *Islamica* 2 (1926): 355–72 (at 370–71). See also F. R. Kraus, "Ein zentrales Problem des altmesopotamischen Rechtes: Was ist der Codex Hammu-rabi?" *Aspects du contact suméro-akkadien* [9th Rencontre assyriologique internationale, Geneva, June 20–23, 1960], *Genava* 8 (1960): 283–96 (at 288, 293); Raymond Westbrook, "Biblical and Cuneiform Law Codes," *Revue biblique* 92 (1985): 247–64; and, especially, Jean Bottéro, *Mesopotamia: Writing, Reasoning, and the Gods* (trans. Zainab Bahrani and Marc Van De Mieroop; Chicago: University of Chicago Press, 1992), 156–84.

4 See Martha T. Roth, "Mesopotamian Legal Traditions and the Laws of Hammurabi," *Chicago-Kent Law Review* 71 (1995): 13–39; Victor Avigdor Hurowitz, "Hammurabi in Mesopotamian Tradition," in *"An Experienced Scribe Who Neglects Nothing": Ancient Near Eastern Studies in Honor of Jacob Klein* (ed. Yitzhak [Yitschak] Sefati et al.; Bethesda, Md.: CDL Press, 2005), 497–532; and, for the most up-to-date list of the copies, Bernard M. Levinson, "Is the Covenant Code an Exilic Composition? A Response to John Van Seters," in idem, *"The Right Chorale": Studies in Biblical Law and Interpretation* (FAT 54; Tübingen: Mohr Siebeck, 2008), 276–330 (at 302).

little direct impact upon subsequent legislation.[5] Even the affective motif of the wronged man being urged, in its epilogue, to consult the stele for redress does not point to a judicial solution but more likely envisions solace in prayer, given the stele's location in the temple.[6] Raymond Westbrook nevertheless attempts to recover some practical role for the literary law collections in actual legal practice. He posits that they "were a reference work for consultation by judges when deciding difficult legal cases." The difficulty, as he properly concedes, is that "there is no direct evidence" to support this hypothesis.[7]

The biblical legal collections share many detailed points of contact with this cuneiform material in technical terminology, formulation, and legal *topos*.[8] In particular, Israelite scribes learned from the cuneiform model the generic convention of framing the series of legal provisions with a literary prologue and epilogue in which a royal

[5] Reuven Yaron, "'Enquire Now about Hammurabi, Ruler of Babylon,'" *The Legal History Review* 59 (1991): 223–38.

[6] Martha T. Roth, "Hammurabi's Wronged Man," *JAOS* 122 (2002): 38–45.

[7] Westbrook, "Law Codes," 254.

[8] See Bernard M. Levinson and Molly M. Zahn, "Revelation Regained: The Hermeneutics of כי and אם in the Temple Scroll," *DSD* 9 (2002): 295–346 (at 301–2; 314–17); David P. Wright, "The Laws of Hammurabi as a Source for the Covenant Collection (Exodus 20:23–23:19)," *Maarav* 10 (2003): 11–87; and Levinson, "Is the Covenant Code an Exilic Composition," 299–304. The evidence is equally strong in terms of Deuteronomy's reception of treaty motifs. The Neo-Assyrian treaty form is presupposed as literary model by Deut 28, perhaps via Aramaic translations; see Hans Ulrich Steymans, *Deuteronomium 28 und die adê zur Thronfolgeregelung Asarhaddons: Segen und Fluch im Alten Orient und in Israel* (OBO 145; Freiburg: Universitätsverlag; Göttingen: Vandenhoeck & Ruprecht, 1995), 143–94.

speaker claims responsibility for promulgating the laws. Using the categories of literary criticism, one might say that these legal collections were given a textual voice by means of such a frame, which put them into the mouth of the reigning monarch. It is not that the divine is unconnected to law in the cuneiform material. Shamash, the Mesopotamian sun god who is the custodian of the cosmic principles of justice, grants King Hammurabi the ability to perceive these eternal truths. Nonetheless, the laws in their actual formulation are royal. Hammurabi repeatedly boasts that the laws are *awâtīya ša ina narîya ašṭuru*, "*my* pronouncements, which *I* have inscribed on *my* stela" (xlix 3–4, 19–21). He refers to them as *awâtīya šūqurātim*, "my precious pronouncements" (xlviii 12–13), and insists, *awâtūa nasqā*, "my pronouncements are choice" (xlviii 99).[9] Confronted by the convention of the royal voicing of law, Israelite authors pushed the genre in a different direction. When King Lear, on the storm-driven heath, was asked by blinded Gloucester for his hand to kiss it in poignant greeting, Lear demurred: "Here, wipe it first; it smells of mortality."[10] As Israelite authors turned their

[9] On this aspect of the Laws of Hammurabi, see the important study of the contrasting ethics of cuneiform and biblical law by Moshe Greenberg, "Some Postulates of Biblical Criminal Law," in *Yehezkel Kaufmann Jubilee Volume* (ed. Menahem Haran; Jerusalem: Magnes, 1960), 5–28; reprinted in idem, *Studies in the Bible and Jewish Thought* (JPS Scholar of Distinction Series; Philadelphia: Jewish Publication Society, 1995), 25–41. In translation, the Laws of Hammurabi are most conveniently available in the excellent edition of Martha T. Roth, *Law Collections from Mesopotamia and Asia Minor* (2d ed.; SBLWAW 6; Atlanta: Scholars Press, 1997), 71–142 (at 134–36).

[10] William Shakespeare, *King Lear* (ed. Stanley Wells, text prepared by Gary Taylor; The Oxford Shakespeare; Oxford: Oxford University Press, 2000), 237 (scene 20, line 128). This edition is based closely

hand to law, they wiped that genre clean of mortality by transforming the royal speaker from a human monarch into their divine king, Yahweh.

With that troping of convention, Israelite scribes introduced into the ancient world a new idea: the divine revelation of law. Accordingly, it was not the legal collection as a literary genre but the voicing of publicly revealed law as the personal will of God that was unique to ancient Israel.[11] That trope of divine revelation had a far-reaching impact upon the literary and intellectual life of ancient Israel. There is a clear relationship between textual voice and textual authority, so that attributing a legal text to God

---

upon the 1608 quarto, which is closest to the original manuscript. Contrast the later, more familiar folio version: "*Let me* wipe it first; it smells of mortality" (4.5.129; emphasis added), as Lear's cohortative ironically inverts Gloucester's eager request: "O, let me kiss that hand!" (4.5.128). For the latter edition, see William Shakespeare, *The Tragedy of King Lear* (ed. Jay L. Halio; The New Cambridge Shakespeare; Cambridge: Cambridge University Press, 1992), 224.

[11] This notion of divine revelation of law constitutes a crucial component of what Karl Jaspers termed the "Axial Age" breakthrough achieved by ancient Israel (*Vom Ursprung und Ziel der Geschichte* [Munich: Piper, 1949], 15–106). See Peter B. Machinist, "On Self-Consciousness in Mesopotamia," in *The Origins and Diversity of Axial Age Civilizations* (ed. Shmuel N. Eisenstadt; Albany: State University of New York Press, 1986), 183–202; idem, "Mesopotamia in Eric Voegelin's *Order and History*," in *Occasional Papers, Eric-Voegelin-Archiv 26* (ed. Peter J. Opitz and Dietmar Herz; Munich: Ludwig-Maximilians University, 2001), 1–54; Jóhann Páll Árnason, "The Axial Age and Its Interpreters: Reopening a Debate," in *Axial Civilizations and World History* (ed. Jóhann Páll Árnason, Shmuel N. Eisenstadt, and Björn Wittrock; Jerusalem Studies in Religion and Culture 4; Leiden: E. J. Brill, 2005), 19–49; Jan Assmann, "Axial 'Breakthroughs' and Semantic 'Relocations' in Ancient Egypt and Israel," in *Axial Civilizations and World History*, 133–56; and Robert N. Bellah, "What is Axial about the Axial Age?" *Archive of European Sociology* 46 (2005): 69–87.

literally gives that text ultimate authority. So strongly was the divine voice privileged as *the* authoritative voice of law that it preempted the emergence to independent dignity of explicitly human legal compositions. Just as there is not a single law in the Bible that Israelite authors do not attribute to God or to his prophetic intermediary, Moses, so does the converse hold true. In the entire Hebrew Bible, not a single text, legal or otherwise, is definitively attributed to the actual scribe responsible for its composition.

Of course, the erasure of the identity of the human author extends far beyond legal texts in the Bible. Except for the prophets, biblical authors never speak explicitly in their own voice. Instead, they employ pseudonyms or write anonymously. Proverbs, for example, is attributed to Solomon by means of its editorial superscription (Prov 1:1), and Ecclesiastes is similarly ascribed to "the son of David, king in Jerusalem" (Qoh 1:1). Neither of these attributions withstands critical examination.[12] Such attributions seem rather to function to lend greater authority or prestige to a literary composition by associating it with a venerable figure from the past: a royal exemplar of the wisdom tradition (1 Kgs 3:28; 4:29–34).

If the notion of divine revelation of law opened up new intellectual and social possibilities, it equally shut down others. The technique of lending ultimate authority to law by attributing it to a divine author raises the question of the

[12] For a summary of the critical issues involved, see J. Alberto Soggin, *Introduction to the Old Testament: From Its Origins to the Closing of the Alexandrian Canon* (3d ed.; OTL; Louisville: Westminster/John Knox Press, 1989), 445–47, 462–64. See further Thomas Krüger, *Qoheleth: A Commentary* (Hermeneia; Minneapolis: Fortress, 2004), 27–28; and Erich Zenger et al., eds., *Einleitung in das Alte Testament* (6th ed.; Kohlhammer Studienbücher Theologie 1.1; Stuttgart: Kohlhammer, 2006), 369.

relative authority of the human legislator. In a legal and literary culture where the divine or prophetic voice has pride of place, what is the place of the human voice? The concept of divine revelation presents special difficulties for the problem of innovation. As noted earlier, in any culture, social, economic, and intellectual change occurs over time. How does a culture with a concept of divine revelation address the problem of legal change? How can legal texts, once viewed as divinely revealed, be revised to fit new circumstances without compromising their—or God's—authority? To make the case of the Bible as distinctive as possible, I will first demonstrate how a neighboring culture lacking the concept of divine revelation resolved the problem of legal change.

The Hittite Laws, arranged on two tablets of one hundred laws each, were discovered in 1906 at Boğazköy in central Turkey. That city had served as the capital of the Hittite Empire, which flourished in Anatolia from approximately 1700–1200 B.C.E.[13] The laws were found in a royal archive. Although originally dating to the middle of the second millennium, they were recopied for several centuries thereafter; the copies actually unearthed date from about 1325–1200 B.C.E. Two aspects of the Hittite Laws make them of particular interest. First, they exist without a literary frame; they thus make no claims whatsoever about the authorship or origins of the legal text.[14] Second—precisely

[13] For a valuable survey, see Trevor Bryce, *The Kingdom of the Hittites* (2d ed.; New York: Oxford University Press, 2006).

[14] For a legal-historical study of the function of the literary frame in cuneiform, biblical, Greek, and Roman laws, see Gerhard Ries, *Prolog und Epilog in Gesetzen des Altertums* (MBPF 76; Munich: C. H. Beck, 1983). It should be noted that some copies of Hammurabi's Code exist without the literary frame; moreover, a version of the prologue

because the laws lack literary voicing—they reveal legal change and development openly. During their long period of recopying, they underwent not only linguistic updating but also revision in the nature and the severity of the penalties they prescribe. The formulation of the laws makes this process of revision explicit.[15] For example, one of the laws governing personal assault reads as follows:[16]

If anyone blinds a free person or knocks his teeth out, *formerly* (*karū*) they would pay 40 sheqels of silver, *but now* (*kinuna*) one pays 20 sheqels of silver . . . (Hittite Laws § 7)

---

has also been discovered without the laws. There has resulted some discussion of which is compositionally prior, the frame or the laws, and whether the combination of the two is original or a result of secondary redaction. Such issues are important to address to determine the literary history and the nature and function of the legal collection within Near Eastern culture. On the redactional relationship between frame and legal corpus, see Jeffrey H. Tigay, "The Stylistic Criterion of Source Criticism in the Light of Ancient Near Eastern and Postbiblical Literature," in *Empirical Models for Biblical Criticism* (ed. Jeffrey H. Tigay; Philadelphia: University of Pennsylvania Press, 1985), 150–73 (at 155–58); and Victor Avigdor Hurowitz, "*Inu Anum ṣīrum*": *Literary Structures in the Non-Juridical Sections of Codex Hammurabi* (Philadelphia: Occasional Publications of the Samuel Noah Kramer Fund 15, 1994), 90–103.

15 On this issue, see Ephraim Neufeld, *The Hittite Laws* (London: Luzac & Co., 1951), 95–101; V. Korošec, "Le problème de la codification dans le domaine du droit hittite," *RIDA* 4 (1957): 93–105; and the articles by Raymond Westbrook ("What is the Covenant Code?"), Samuel Greengus ("Some Issues Relating to the Comparability of Laws and the Coherence of the Legal Tradition"), and Eckart Otto ("Aspects of Legal Reforms and Reformulations in Ancient Cuneiform and Israelite Law"), in *Theory and Method in Biblical and Cuneiform Law: Revision, Interpolation and Development* (ed. Bernard M. Levinson; JSOTSup 181; Sheffield: Sheffield Academic Press, 1994; reprint, Sheffield: Sheffield Phoenix, 2006), 22–28, 62–72, 175–82.

16 My translation departs slightly from that in the excellent recent edition by Harry Angier Hoffner Jr., *The Laws of the Hittites: A Critical Edition* (DMOA 23; Leiden: E. J. Brill, 1997), 21.

The legal speaker makes a clear distinction between what was formerly the case and what is now the case, between what would have been done and what is currently the practice. This opposition is marked grammatically: there is a shift from the durative-iterative form of the verb to the present tense. The new fine is only half the original one. The same formula is used to revise twenty-three of the two hundred Hittite Laws, or nearly 12 percent of them.[17] The changes marked by the "formerly . . . but now" formula derive from a far-reaching legal reform, carried out under King Telipinu (ca. 1525–1500 B.C.E.), of a version of the laws codified a century or two earlier in the Hittite Old Kingdom.[18] Moreover, the revision and updating of older law continued to occur after the codification of this text. A later copy, prepared a century or two afterward, further reduces or revises the fines, while also reorganizing the sequence of some of the laws. This updated version, however, deletes all reference to the older penalties; they are simply ignored as obsolete.[19] In this version, the fine for

[17] This formula occurs in the Hittite Laws §§ 7, 9, 19, 25, 51, 54, 57, 58, 59, 63, 67, 69, 81, 91, 92, 94, 101, 119, 121, 122, 123 (fragmentary text), 129, and 166–67. Note the valuable discussion of the formula in Hoffner, *Laws of the Hittites*, 5–7. For suggestive parallels to the Hittite formulary in rabbinic and Roman law, see Martin S. Jaffee, "The Taqqanah in Tannaitic Literature: Jurisprudence and the Construction of Rabbinic Memory," *JJS* 41 (1990): 204–25.

[18] Hoffner, *Laws of the Hittites*, 221.

[19] Most valuable is the edition by Richard Haase, which presents this latest version of the laws separately, as an independent work; see idem, *Die Keilschriftlichen Rechtssammlungen in deutscher Fassung* (2d ed.; Wiesbaden: Otto Harrassowitz, 1979), 67–91. The more common form of publication obscures the independence of that version by blending it back into the earlier version that it seeks to update and replace. What results is an "eclectic text" that never existed in antiquity, whereby the later version's individual stipulations are appended to the pertinent ones of the main version, and identified

knocking the teeth out has been reduced to twelve sheqels, and a class distinction has been introduced: if the injured party is a slave, the fine is only half that amount.[20]

If legal amendment repeatedly manifests itself within a century or two of the original codification of the Hittite Laws, similar kinds of revision would naturally be expected to have taken place in ancient Israel, whose literature spans nearly one thousand years.[21] The wrenching shifts in economy, social structure, political organization, and religion that Israel underwent in this period only increase the likelihood that legal amendment should have occurred. Nonetheless, the Hebrew Bible reveals a remarkable absence of explicit evidence for the revision and updating of pentateuchal law. There are four cases within the Pentateuch of new divine oracles, mediated by Moses, that supplement the existing provisions of covenantal law with judicial adjustments to unforeseen circumstances (Lev 24:10–23; Num 9:6–14; 15:32–36; 27:1–11).

as "Late(r) Version." Such is the approach of Albrecht Goetze, trans., "The Hittite Laws," in *Ancient Near Eastern Texts Relating to the Old Testament* (ed. James B. Pritchard; 3d ed.; Princeton, N.J.: Princeton University Press, 1969), 188–97; and Hoffner, *Laws of the Hittites.*

20 See Hoffner, *Laws of the Hittites*, 22 (§ VII).

21 The dating of the biblical literary sources is complex. The dates here extend from the Yahwist, often considered the oldest documentary source of the Pentateuch (but now deemed by many scholars actually to be exilic or postexilic), to the book of Daniel, the latest book to enter the canon of the Hebrew Bible. For trends in the dating and analysis of biblical literature, see *The Hebrew Bible and Its Modern Interpreters* (ed. Douglas A. Knight and Gene M. Tucker; SBLBMI 1; Philadelphia: Fortress Press; Chico, Calif.: Scholars Press, 1985); and Ronald Hendel, "Appendix: Linguistic Notes on the Age of Biblical Literature," in *Remembering Abraham: Culture, Memory, and History in the Hebrew Bible* (New York: Oxford University Press, 2005), 109–64.

In these instances, the earlier law is not revoked; instead, given particular unforeseen eventualities, a divine oracle is represented as allowing Moses to render a judgment. The very ad hoc nature of these situations makes them the exception that proves the rule.[22] The one clear case of explicit legal revision in the Hebrew Bible, found in the book of Ruth, deals not with revealed law but with custom—and even the custom may be a romantic construction with little foundation in legal history. This case is nonetheless worth exploring here, because it demonstrates how the very idea of legal history, whether asserted or denied, may frequently represent a literary trope that is constructed by authors.

LEGAL HISTORY AS A LITERARY TROPE IN RUTH

The superscription to the book of Ruth places it in the ancient period of the Israelite settlement in Canaan, prior to the emergence of the monarchy: "in the days when the judges ruled" (Ruth 1:1). That superscription almost certainly accounts for the book's being placed by the Septuagint (and thus, still, in Catholic and Protestant Bibles) immediately after the book of Judges, so as literally to come before the introduction of the monarchy (1–2 Samuel).

[22] For an astute analysis of these passages, see Michael Fishbane, *Biblical Interpretation in Ancient Israel* (2d ed.; Oxford: Clarendon, 1988), 98–102; and Simeon Chavel, "Law and Narrative in Four Oracular Novellae in the Pentateuch: Lev 24:10–23; Num 9:1–14; 15:32–36; 27:1–11," Ph.D. diss., Hebrew University of Jerusalem, 2006 (Hebrew); revised as *Oracular Law and Narrative History: The Priestly Literature of the Pentateuch* (FAT series 2; Tübingen: Mohr Siebeck, forthcoming in 2009).

Despite its narrative setting in antiquity, most scholars would date Ruth, on the basis of its language, to the postexilic period of the reconstruction, when, under Persian sovereignty, there was no longer a Judean monarchy.[23]

To be sure, many scholars consider the matter of language alone not to be decisive for the dating. Additional evidence also points to the postexilic period as the most logical home for the composition of the text. Georg Braulik demonstrates the extent to which the book of Ruth depends upon and reinterprets legal material in the Pentateuch, drawing upon the legal corpus of Deuteronomy in particular.[24] From this perspective, Ruth emerges as

23 See Jean-Luc Vesco, "La date du livre de Ruth," *RB* 74 (1967): 235–47 (at 245–47). For a useful survey of the history of research, see Robert L. Hubbard, *The Book of Ruth* (NICOT; Grand Rapids, Mich.: William B. Eerdmans, 1988), 23–35. Maintaining a Josianic date (just prior to the exile) and providing a valuable survey of the issues is Jack M. Sasson, *Ruth: A New Translation with a Philological Commentary and a Formalist-Folklorist Interpretation* (2d ed.; Sheffield: Sheffield Academic Press, 1989), 240–52. More compelling, however, are the arguments for a postexilic setting in the Persian period. See Christian Frevel, *Das Buch Rut* (Neuer Stuttgarter Kommentar, Altes Testament 6; Stuttgart: Katholisches Bibelwerk, 1992), 34; and Yair Zakovitch, *Das Buch Rut: Ein jüdischer Kommentar* (SBS 177; Stuttgart: Katholisches Bibelwerk, 1999), 38–40. See also the succinct summary of the arguments in favor of a date in the fifth century B.C.E. ("wohl im 5. Jr.") provided by Erich Zenger, "Das Buch Rut," in *Einleitung in das Alte Testament* (ed. Erich Zenger et al.; 6th ed.; Kohlhammer Studienbücher Theologie 1.1; Stuttgart: Kohlhammer, 2006), 222–29 (at 226). Here Zenger seems discretely to modify his earlier proposal for a Hellenistic setting in the second century B.C.E.; see Erich Zenger, *Das Buch Ruth* (2d ed.; ZBKAT 8; Zürich: Theologischer Verlag, 1992), 28.

24 Georg Braulik, "Das Deuteronomium und die Bücher Ijob, Sprichwörter und Rut: Zur Frage früher Kanonizität des Deuteronomiums," in idem, *Studien zum Deuteronomium und seiner Nachgeschichte* (SBAB 33; Stuttgart: Katholisches, 2001), 213–93

more than a beautiful if naive ancient folktale or "romantic idyll."[25] Instead, it constitutes something closer to a counter-narrative that seeks to revise and liberalize the requirements of Deuteronomy regarding gleaning rules (Deut 24:19), the exclusion of Moabites from the community (Deut 23:4–5 [English, 23:3–4]); and the laws of levirate marriage (Deut 25:5–10).[26] The details of those arguments cannot be rehearsed here. Nonetheless, the model where by the book of Ruth, in each of its chapters, may be understood as inner-biblical exegesis of the community, family, and social justice laws of Deuteronomy 23–25 points to the postexilic period as the most logical context for the book's composition.[27]

From that vantage point, the literary setting of Ruth represents an attempt at conscious archaizing. The literary technique of presenting a contemporary literary

(at 258–80); and idem, in an abridged translation of the original publication of the preceding, "The Book of Ruth as Intra-Biblical Critique of the Deuteronomic Law," *AcT* 19 (1999): 1–20. A similar approach is taken by Joshua Berman, for whom the plot of Ruth "unfolds according to the sequential order of the legal material in Deuteronomy 24,16–25,10" ("Ancient Hermeneutics and the Legal Structure of the Book of Ruth," *ZAW* 119 [2007]: 22–38 [at 23]). Berman does not draw, at least not in explicit terms, the implications of his fine analysis for the book's dating.

[25] Contra Zakovitch, *Das Buch Rut*, 11: "idyllisch-romantisch."

[26] Only by overlooking such crucial legal matters and restricting himself to narrative elements can Arndt Meinhold place the composition of Ruth in the early preexilic period, prior to Deuteronomy, as a document of Bethlehemite tradition ("Theologische Schwerpunkte im Buch Ruth und ihr Gewicht für seine Datierung," *TZ* 32 [1976]: 129–37).

[27] "Ruth is the only Biblical example of an *entire* book systematically subjecting regulations of the Deuteronomic code to a socio-critical (Rt 1–2) and sexual-critical (Rt 3–4) *relecture* by allusions of different kinds" (Braulik, "Book of Ruth as Intra-Biblical Critique," 18).

composition as if it were ancient, both in narrative form and in imitation of earlier language, is well known in the Second Temple period. It is especially associated with the Chronicler.[28] Similar literary techniques are also evident in classical antiquity.[29] The theme of the book (the integration of a Moabite into Israel by means of marriage) engages a much larger debate concerning ethnicity and identity reflected within literature of the Second Temple period. Other texts, set explicitly in the Persian period, show how contested and divisive such issues were, as those who returned from exile sought to constitute themselves as a new Israel organized around a rebuilt Temple. Ezra and Nehemiah, for example, draw a firm boundary line of ethnicity around the emergent community. They take an exclusivist stance, urging expulsion of foreigners, rejecting integration through marriage (Ezra 9–10).[30] If Ezra's

28 Demonstrating that this applies to the account of the reorganization of justice in 2 Chronicles 19, which many scholars had long assumed to be an ancient text, and proving that it casts a programmatic late conception into the past, see Alexander Rofé, "The Strata about the Organization of Justice in Deuteronomy (16:18–20; 17:8–13)," *Beth Miqra* 65 (1976): 199–210 (Hebrew; English abstract); and Gary N. Knoppers, "Jehoshaphat's Judiciary and 'the Scroll of YHWH's Torah,'" *JBL* 113 (1994): 59–80. Published in Hebrew, Rofé's article has been widely overlooked in the field. It has recently been updated and translated. See "The Organization of the Judiciary in Deuteronomy (16.18–20; 17.8–13; 19.15; 21.22–23; 24.16; 25.1–3)," in idem, *Deuteronomy: Issues and Interpretation* (OTS; London: T. & T. Clark, 2002), 103–19.

29 For a similar process in Greek literature, see the treatment in James I. Porter, "Feeling Classical: Classicism and Ancient Literary Criticism," in *Classical Pasts: The Classical Traditions of Greece and Rome* (ed. James I. Porter; Princeton, N.J.: Princeton University Press, 2006), 301–52 (esp. 316–23).

30 See Fishbane, *Biblical Interpretation*, 114–29. For a valuable analysis of these issues from a social-scientific perspective, see David Janzen, *Witch-Hunts, Purity, and Social Boundaries: The Expulsion of*

policies are tendentiously cast as the intent of ancient scriptural tradition, so too do the policies of Ruth's authors receive the warrant of ancient tradition: they are framed as an ancient folktale, set in the period of the Israelite settlement. In contrast to Ezra's exclusionist stance, however, the authors of the book of Ruth promote a porous view of the community's boundaries, sanctioning inclusion through marriage.[31] This policy receives final warrant in the genealogy that concludes the book: David—the founder of a dynasty, and Israel's greatest king—is the son of Jesse, the issue of this marriage between Israelite Boaz and Moabite Ruth (Ruth 4:17–22). The literary setting of Ruth thus represents an argument addressed to a postexilic audience about the boundaries of the community. Narrative time here serves as a literary trope in support of an argument about ethnicity and cultural identity.

At a pivotal point in the plot, the historical distance between the book's literary setting and the actual date of its composition (and thus of its intended readership) becomes clear. Boaz cannot legally marry Ruth until a nearer kinsman publicly surrenders his prior claim. Boaz thus calls this kinsman to a legal ceremony held before the elders at the village gate, the traditional site of public justice

the Foreign Women in Ezra 9–10 (JSOTSup 350; Sheffield: Sheffield Academic Press, 2002).

[31] Prophetic literature enters into the same debate. Ezekiel 44 advances an exclusivist position, while Trito-Isaiah argues for the inclusion of the foreigner within the community (Isa 56:3–8). For discussions of the "clash of interpretations" represented by Ezek 44:6–9 and Isa 56:4–7, see Fishbane, *Biblical Interpretation*, 138–43; and Joachim Schaper, "Rereading the Law: Inner-Biblical Exegesis of Divine Oracles in Ezekiel 44 and Isaiah 56," in *Recht und Ethik im Alten Testament: Studies in German and English in Honor of Gerhard von Rad* (ed. Bernard M. Levinson and Eckart Otto, with assistance from Walter Dietrich; ATM 13; Münster: LIT Verlag, 2004), 125–44.

in the ancient Near East.[32] The details of the ceremony are presented in a chess-like verbal exchange whereby Boaz first invites the kinsman to exercise his right to redeem an ancestral plot of land, without mentioning Ruth's existence. The solicitation secures the kinsman's initial interest (Ruth 4:3–4a). Only after the kinsman confirms his intent to acquire the land does Boaz reveal the rub: were the kinsman to assert the right of redemption of ancestral land, he is also obliged, consistent with the rules of levirate marriage, to espouse Ruth, Naomi's daughter-in-law (Ruth 4:5). But the convention of levirate marriage is that the progeny continue the line and the estate of the deceased husband, not of the new husband, or *levir*.

Faced thereby with economic double jeopardy—he would disadvantage himself by purchasing land that would

[32] On the village gate as the site of public trials (note also Deut 21:19; 22:15; 25:7), see Victor H. Matthews, "Entrance Ways and Threshing Floors: Legally Significant Sites in the Ancient Near East," *Fides et Historia* 19 (1987): 25–40; and Eckart Otto, "שער *Šaʿar*," *ThWAT* (Stuttgart: Kohlhammer, 1995): 8:358–403. For the role of the elders in the administration of justice, see Moshe Weinfeld, "Elders," in *Encyclopaedia Judaica* (Jerusalem: Encyclopaedia Judaica, 1972), 6:578–80; Leslie J. Hoppe, *The Origins of Deuteronomy* (Ann Arbor, Mich.: University Microfilms, 1978); idem, "Elders and Deuteronomy," *EgT* 14 (1983): 259–72; Joachim Buchholz, *Die Ältesten Israels im Deuteronomium* (GTA 36; Göttingen: Vandenhoeck & Ruprecht, 1988); Jan Christian Gertz, *Die Gerichtsorganisation Israels im deuteronomischen Gesetz* (FRLANT 165; Göttingen: Vandenhoeck & Ruprecht, 1994), 173–225; Hanoch Reviv, *The Elders in Ancient Israel: A Study of a Biblical Institution* (Jerusalem: Magnes, 1989), 61–70 (whose analysis, however, does not address essential diachronic issues); Bernard M. Levinson, *Deuteronomy and the Hermeneutics of Legal Innovation* (New York: Oxford University Press, 1997), 124–26; and Timothy M. Willis, *The Elders of the City: A Study of the Elders-Laws in Deuteronomy* (SBLMS 55; Atlanta: Society of Biblical Literature, 2001).

paradoxically not increase his estate but rather transfer out of it—the kinsman declines the offer. As intended, he cedes the right of land redemption—and thus of marriage—to Boaz.[33] Just at this climax of the negotiations, an editor arrests the drama to observe:

> Thus *formerly* (לפנים) it was done in Israel in cases of redemption or exchange: to validate any transaction, one man *would* take off his sandal and hand it to the other. Such was the practice in Israel. (Ruth 4:7)

Immediately following this meta-commentary on the dramatic action, whereby the narrator boldly inserts his own voice, the plot moves rapidly forward to its conclusion. It integrates all the players and assigns them a new identity, as if at the end of a Shakespearean comedy upon the return from the forest: Boaz agrees to redeem the land (4:9) and he agrees to serve as *levir* and acquire Ruth as his wife (4:10).

33 The connection between the law of land redemption (Lev 25:25–28; reflected also in Jer 34:8–22) and that of levirate marriage (Deut 25:5–10; cf. Gen 38:1–11) is that both share the common goal of retaining ancestral land within the clan and preventing its alienation through sale or marriage. These issues are assumed in the narrative of Ruth 4. By choosing to redeem the land, the nearer kinsman would return the property to the family and thus reactivate the possibility of continuing the dead man's line. Because the deceased's widow, Ruth, still survives, the kinsman as closest relative would be expected to assume the role of *levir* and thus of producing children for the deceased (Gen 38:9), to whom the redeemed property would transfer as their rightful inheritance. Although the kinsman is still technically the *levir* even before the land is redeemed, there is no point in raising children for the deceased in the absence of property for them to inherit. The deceased's "name" (cf. Deut 25:6–7) is tied to the hereditary property and is lost without it (Ruth 4:5, 10). For a lucid analysis, see Raymond Westbrook, *Property and the Family in Biblical Law* (JSOTSup 113; Sheffield: Sheffield Academic Press, 1991), 65–67.

Most remarkably, the elders bless this union. They wholeheartedly welcome the Moabite, Ruth—who according to pentateuchal law would have been unconditionally and perpetually barred from entering the community of Israel (Deut 23:4). Moreover they affirm her as a prospective Israelite matriarch and builder of the community: "May Yahweh make the woman who is coming into your house like Rachel and Leah, both of whom built up the House of Israel!" (Ruth 4:11). The elders' wish is quickly fulfilled with, the narrator stresses, divine support (4:13). If it took four chapters to reach this point in the narrative, it takes but four verses for Boaz and Ruth to marry, cohabit, and bear and name the child of that union. That child will indeed contribute profoundly to the House of Israel. His grandson is destined to become the founder of the United Monarchy. So anxious is the narrator to make this clear that he intrudes into the scene and steals the words out of the mouth of his own characters. No sooner does he recount that "the women" (presumably neighbor women assisting at the birth, as at 4:14) celebrate the successful delivery by naming the child than he truncates the continuation of their speech to breathlessly announce both name and fame himself: "The women [neighbors] gave him a name, saying, 'A son is born to Naomi!' *They named him Obed; he was the father of Jesse, father of David.*" (4:17)

The rapid denouement follows from the narrator's meta-commentary on the ceremony involving the removal of the sandal just cited (4:7); that moment functions as a turning point in the plot. The narrator's comment calls attention to itself: it marks the intrusion of the narrator's own voice and also the intrusion of a temporal perspective inconsistent with the narrative time of the story being told. The comment addresses a different audience that is extrinsic to the לפנים, "formerly," of the story and who live subsequent to its time and follow a different set of legal protocols to mark the conclusion of contracts. But with so much riding on what follows, why does this comment occur at all? Why intrude into the narrative time of the tale with a different perspective? Why does the narrator place the plot on hold to treat the symbolic legal action as a museum piece that requires historical explanation, thereby risking the breakdown of any sense of narrative verisimilitude or chronological consistency?

There are two possible models of explanation. The first interprets the text literally, seeing the insertion as explaining a real custom from older times. Whereas the whole book ostensibly presents a story from ancient times, this one item would have been unfamiliar and in need of special clarification. That approach, which I previously also advanced, views the verse as a later editor's insertion.[34] It assumes that a symbolic legal ritual of removing the sandal to mark the conclusion of an oral contract must once have existed and since fallen into disuse.[35] The annotation is inserted into the narrative for the benefit of the text's contemporary reader, who would otherwise have found the archaic ritual unintelligible. Indeed, linguistic analysis of

34 See Wilhelm Rudolph, *Das Buch Ruth; das Hohe Lied; die Klagelieder* (KAT 17.1–3; Gütersloh: Gerd Mohn, 1962), 67–68; Frevel, *Rut*, 138 (although recognizing it as archaizing); and Bernard M. Levinson, "'You Must Not Add Anything to What I Command You': Paradoxes of Canon and Authorship in Ancient Israel," *Numen* 50 (2003): 1–51 (at 22–23).

35 The technical force of the formula in Hebrew, especially clear from the parallel in 1 Sam 9:9, has been noted by E. F. Campbell Jr., *Ruth* (AB 7; Garden City, N.Y.: Doubleday, 1975), 147–48.

the annotation confirms its late date and its inconsistency with the literary setting of the narrative.[36]

The second interpretation presents the text as a series of Chinese boxes. It is the narrator, in his narrative art, who constructs the custom as an obsolete ancient one. The reader is still presented with what appears to be an ancient custom. But the narrator here, unlike in the first hypothesis, is not providing a scholastic comment upon an antique museum piece or entering into the narrative world of the story from the position of hindsight. Instead, the narrator is creating a deliberate literary fiction designed to couch his legal revisions as legitimate ancient traditions. He still needs an explanation at 4:7 for a custom unfamiliar to his audience, but the custom in this view is cut from whole cloth. The advantage of this more complex model is that it seems much truer to what I think can correctly be said about the composition of the book of Ruth as a whole: that the entire book represents a composition of the Second Temple period.

From that vantage point, the comment at 4:7 makes little sense as a later editor's interpolation, when the entire narrative represents a late composition. Relegating that annotation alone to the Second Temple period as a late addition to the book, on the basis of its language, as if the Second Temple elements in Ruth were safely restricted to that verse alone, is methodologically naive. As has often

[36] Establishing the exilic/postexilic date of the editorial insertion by means of careful linguistic analysis, see Avi Hurvitz, "On the Term שלף נעל in Ruth 4:7," in *Shnaton I: An Annual for Biblical and Ancient Near Eastern Studies* (ed. Jonas C. Greenfield and Moshe Weinfeld; Jerusalem: Israel Bible Company; Tel Aviv: M. Newman; 1975), 45–49 (Hebrew; English abstract, pp. xiii–xiv).

been noted, the ritual in Ruth bears no direct analogue to anything in the Pentateuch. In the levirate law of Deut 25: 5–10, it is the widow who removes the shoe of her brother-in-law who has refused his duty, spits in his face, and makes solemn declaration.[37] The situation in Ruth is "diametrically opposed": here, it is the man himself who removes his shoe (in each case, a different Hebrew verb is employed) to confirm the relinquishing of a right (not the refusal of a duty) and there is no spitting.[38]

Ruth is a postexilic composition that stages its narrative in the premonarchic past. It therefore makes more sense to view the annotation not as later editor's insertion into a preexisting narrative but as part of the author's coherent literary strategy of archaizing. The annotation creates the perception of a chronological gap between the literary present of the narrator and audience, on the one hand, and the ostensibly preliterary past of the characters in the narrative, on the other. This has less to do with legal history than with literary history. The challenge to and bypassing of the pentateuchal law that perpetually bars the Moabite and the Ammonite and their descendants from membership in the Israelite community (Deut 23:4 [English 23:3]) is thus located in the venerable

37 For a good overview, see Åke Viberg, *Symbols of Law: A Contextual Analysis of Legal Symbolic Acts in the Old Testament* (ConBOT 34; Stockholm: Almqvist & Wiksell International, 1992), 145–48; and, drawing on anthropological theory, Paul A. Kruger, "The Removal of the Sandal in Deuteronomy XXV 9: 'A Rite of Passage'?" *VT* 46 (1996): 534–39.

38 Braulik, "Book of Ruth as Intra-Biblical Critique," 17. See further the stimulating commentary by Irmtraud Fischer, *Rut* (2d ed.; HThKAT; Freiburg: Herder, 2005), 61, 241–44 (who also identifies the function of the shoe ritual).

past. The formal marking of the ritual that seals the legal transaction as ancient, precisely by emphasizing that it no longer is current "nowadays," heightens the perception of its authenticity. The step-by-step sequence that leads to the transformation of Ruth from foreigner (Moabite) to the Israelite wife of Boaz and thence to matriarch of the line of Jesse, and thereby directly to David (Ruth 4:17–22) carries the weight of venerable tradition. If this past does not go back to the literary time assigned Moses in Deuteronomy (on the steppes of Moab!), it nonetheless is located in the period of the settlement and associated with a union that claims King David as its direct issue. In deriving the legendary founder of the United Monarchy itself from such a union, it becomes clear the extent to which Ruth's assumptions about Israelite identity (the legal and religious status of foreigners, ethnicity, and intermarriage) offers a very different vision of the community and its boundaries than that articulated in Ezra and Nehemiah. Yet the narrative never directly presents itself as a counter-narrative. Still less does it explicitly take issue with Deuteronomic law (intermarriage, admission of Moabites into the community).

This example from Ruth is the single explicit acknowledgement in the Bible of a legal modification. The technical formula distinguishes between what was formerly the case and what is implicitly now the case: "Thus *formerly* it was done in Israel in cases of redemption or exchange: to validate any transaction, one man *would* take off his sandal and hand it to the other. Such was the practice in Israel" (Ruth 4:7). The annotation recalls the almost identically formulated opposition in the Hittite Laws, discussed earlier, that "*formerly* they *would* pay 40 sheqels of silver but now one pays 20 sheqels." The analysis of the latter case made it possible to see how inevitable legal change can be directly addressed in a legal collection that lacks either literary voicing or direct attribution to a prestigious divine or royal speaker. The case of Ruth, while formally similar, points in a different direction. The symbolic legal ritual, like the past in which it is embedded, represents a strategic literary fiction. The representation of the past, along with the allusions to the legal protocols (levirate marriage, land acquisition, formalization of legal transactions), is a romanticized construction with scant foundation in legal history. Embedded in a legal narrative, it already begins to point to the complexities involved in the reformulation of pentateuchal law. Here, legal history emerges as something closer to a literary trope and an authorial strategy. The actual literary history of Ruth in relation to its precursor texts, as it constructs new law and recasts old law, is deflected. It is only an unwritten common law or old custom, nothing more, that has fallen into disuse, certainly not Deuteronomy's stipulations concerning ethnicity and identity.

THE IMPACT OF THE IDEA OF DIVINE REVELATION

An entirely new set of literary and religious issues emerges with the pentateuchal claim that its laws originate in divine revelation. Strikingly, biblical authors do at times represent God as fallible. He is so taken aback by the immorality of his creation that, in a remarkable soliloquy at the outset of the biblical flood story, he reveals his fallibility: "Yahweh said, 'I will blot out from the earth humankind whom I have created—from humans to cattle to creeping things to birds of the sky; for I regret that I made them'" (Gen 6:7; cf. 6:6).[39] In other cases as well, Yahweh concedes his fallibility, or at least the absence of omniscience, and is forced to change his plans as a result of human iniquity (1 Sam 2:30; 15:11; note also, inconsistently, 1 Sam 15:29). Even divine oracles proclaimed by the prophets sometimes remained unfulfilled or were controverted by history, a problem that the editors of the prophetic books were forced to address.[40] For example, contrary to earlier oracles against Tyre and Sidon (Ezek 26:1–28:24, esp. 26:7–14), the Babylonian king Nebuchadnezzar was unable to destroy Tyre, despite laying siege to the city. The prophet Ezekiel acknowledges the failure of the original oracle by referencing the failed siege against Tyre in a corrective oracle that now, by way of substitution, promises the Babylonian king Egypt "as the wages for his army . . . as his payment for which he [Nebuchadnezzar] labored . . ." (Ezek 29:19–20).[41]

Another perspective makes it possible to triangulate the argument that, within the Pentateuch, biblical law is rhetorically constructed to be infallible and error free. There is a remarkable tradition preserved by the prophet

[39] See my study, "'The Right Chorale': From the Poetics of Biblical Narrative to the Hermeneutics of the Hebrew Bible," in idem, "*The Right Chorale*"*: Studies in Biblical Law and Interpretation* (FAT 54; Tübingen: Mohr Siebeck, 2008), 7–39 (at 17–18); and Jean-Pierre Sonnet, "God's Repentance and 'False Starts' in Biblical History," in *Congress Volume Ljubljana 2007* (ed. André Lemaire; VTSup; Leiden: E. J. Brill, forthcoming in 2009).

[40] The first to recognize this issue was Robert P. Carroll, *When Prophecy Failed: Reactions to Failure in the Old Testament Prophetic Traditions* (London: SCM Press, 1979).

[41] For this and other examples, see Fishbane, *Biblical Interpretation*, 476–77.

Ezekiel, in the context of a divine diatribe against Israel for its apostasy: "And I also gave them laws not good and rules by which they could not live by, defiling them by their gifts, in that they delivered up every first issue of the womb, so that I might desolate them, so that they might know that I am YHWH" (Ezek 20:25–26). But even here, in the fierceness of the prophetic polemic, the idea seems to be that, in retaliation for the people's consistent rejection of God's originally good laws, he implemented the opposite, as a form of measure-for-measure punishment. Moshe Greenberg puts the matter well: "By this anti-gift God only confirmed the people in their choice of laws countering God's."[42]

In none of these cases, however, is there any question about the infallibility of the divine laws or ethical proclamations themselves, which are the focus here. In a sense, God's fallibility, as the flood story reveals, is that he has created a fallible humanity. For just this reason, prophetic visions of a postexilic "new age" often include notions of the inauguration of a new moral and religious regime. Such visions often include formulae that distinguish current practice from future transformation: for example, "In those [future] days, no longer shall they say . . . but rather . . . " (Jer 3:16; 23:7–8; 31:29–30; cf. 16:14–15; Ezek 18:2). The new regime nonetheless presupposes

[42] Moshe Greenberg, *Ezekiel 1–20* (AB 22; Garden City, N.Y.: Doubleday, 1983), 361 (the translation) and 369 (the citation). Taking this issue a step further, see Rainer Kessler, "'Gesetze, die nicht gut waren' (Ez 20,25)—eine Polemik gegen das Deuteronomium," in *Schriftprophetie: Festschrift für Jörg Jeremias zum 65. Geburtstag* (ed. Friedhelm Hartenstein, Jutta Krispenz, and Aaron Schart; Neukirchen-Vluyn: Neukirchener Verlag, 2004), 253–63.

the continuing validity of divine law. The change lies in the divine reprogramming of human nature, as if to enable—or perhaps coerce—fallible humans to heed God's infallible law: "I will set my Torah within them; upon their heart will I write it" (Jer 31:33; similarly, Ezek 36:27).[43]

Thus despite biblical narrators' portrayal of God as changing his mind, making mistakes, making adjustments, and expressing regret, the authors of legal documents choose to portray God's wisdom and authority as absolute. Once a law is attributed to God, it cannot be questioned or qualified. Can one imagine a human editor candidly emerging from the text, as in Ruth, now, however, to announce the obsolescence of a divine commandment? There clearly exists an inherent tension within the biblical laws between renewal and conservatism: between the need to amend laws or create new ones in light of inevitable historical change and the desire to preserve the authority of laws claiming a divine origin.[44]

As a result of this tension, it was necessary to develop a number of sophisticated literary strategies to present new law as not in fact involving the revision or annulment of older laws. The biblical authors developed what may best be described as a rhetoric of concealment, one that served to camouflage the actual literary history of the laws. The revision of old law and the creation of new law continued

43 See Moshe Weinfeld, "Jeremiah and the Spiritual Metamorphosis of Israel," *ZAW* 88 (1976): 17–55.

44 Martin Noth, *Die Welt des Alten Testaments: Einführung in die Grenzgebiete der alttestamentlichen Wissenschaft* (4th ed.; Sammlung Töpelmann 2/3; Berlin: Alfred Töpelmann, 1962), 267. See also Christoph Levin, *Die Verheißung des neuen Bundes: in ihrem theologiegeschichtlichen Zusammenhang ausgelegt* (FRLANT 137; Göttingen: Vandenhoeck & Ruprecht, 1985), 68–69.

to occur, just as in the Hittite Laws. But rather than candidly specify, "this law is no longer the case," the editor of divine laws found indirect ways to adapt old law to new circumstances without slighting the prestige or authority of laws that tradition ascribed to divine revelation. We have seen, in the previous section, how the legal narrative of Ruth embedded a romanticized legal history as a literary trope in its effort to authorize new law. In what follows, I demonstrate a range of literary strategies that biblical authors employed to authorize—and to conceal—such reworking.

The Decalogue, which symbolizes the Israelite concept of revelation, provides a ready point of departure for examining these strategies.[45] In the second of its

45 This point of departure should be seen more in heuristic than in historical terms. It is difficult to place the Decalogue in its present form at the beginning of the history of Israelite religion or to consider it ancient. This difficulty besets the otherwise excellent exegetical treatment by Moshe Weinfeld, "The Decalogue: Its Significance, Uniqueness, and Place in Israel's Tradition," in *Religion and Law: Biblical-Judaic and Islamic Perspectives* (ed. Edwin Brown Firmage, Bernard G. Weiss, and John W. Welch; Winona Lake, Ind.: Eisenbrauns, 1990), 3–47. His approach, which regards the Decalogue as ancient and Mosaic in origin, should be supplemented by the evidence for a late Deuteronomistic redaction of the Sinai pericope. See, e.g., Reinhard G. Kratz, "Der Dekalog im Exodusbuch," *VT* 44 (1994): 205–38; Erich Zenger, "Wie und wozu die Tora zum Sinai kam: Literarische und theologische Beobachtungen zu Exodus 19–34," in *Studies in the Book of Exodus: Redaction-Reception-Interpretation* (ed. Marc Vervenne; BETL 126; Leuven: University Press/Peeters Press, 1996), 265–88; idem, "Der Stand der Dekalogforschung," in *Recht und Ethik im Alten Testament* (ed. Bernard M. Levinson and Eckart Otto, with assistance from Walter Dietrich; ATM 13; Münster/London: LIT Verlag, 2004), 57–65; and Matthias Köckert, "Wie kam das Gesetz an den Sinai?" in *Vergegenwärtigung des Alten Testaments: Beiträge zur biblischen Hermeneutik für Rudolf*

commandments, God affirms his zeal for an intimate and exclusive relationship with Israel.[46] In its present context, that commandment begins with a prohibition: "You shall not make for yourself *an idol*, whether in the form of anything that is in the heavens above or the earth below or in the waters beneath the earth" (Exod 20:4). After that singular grammatical object, the following verse extends the initial prohibition, yet, apparently ungrammatically, assumes a plural rather than a singular antecedent: "You shall not bow down to *them* or worship *them*" (Exod 20:5).[47] The lack of grammatical agreement raises the possibility that there has been a textual disturbance. The plural pronouns of verse 5 seem most logically to refer back to the first

---

Smend zum 70. Geburtstag (ed. Christoph Bultmann, Walter Dietrich, and Christoph Levin; Göttingen: Vandenhoeck & Ruprecht, 2002), 13–27. For a different approach, see Christoph Levin, "Der Dekalog am Sinai," in idem, *Fortschreibungen: Gesammelte Studien zum Alten Testament* (BZAW 316; New York: Walter de Gruyter, 2003), 60–80.

46 In antiquity, different systems of enumerating the Decalogue were employed by rabbinic Judaism, Hellenistic Judaism, and the church fathers. As a result, differences show up still in the Jewish, Catholic, Orthodox, and Protestant enumerations. Within the Jewish tradition itself, two different systems for punctuating and organizing the Hebrew text of the commandments are provided simultaneously (an upper and a lower system). On these issues, see Mordechai Breuer, "Dividing the Decalogue into Verses and Commandments," in *The Ten Commandments in History and Tradition* (ed. Ben-Zion Segal; trans. Gershon Levi; Jerusalem: Magnes Press, 1990), 291–330. For a schematic overview, see Bernard M. Levinson, "Deuteronomy: Introduction and Commentary," in *The Jewish Study Bible* (ed. Adele Berlin and Marc Zvi Brettler; New York: Oxford University Press, 2003), 356–450 (at 374–76).

47 First identifying this redactional issue, see Walther Zimmerli, "Das zweite Gebot" [1950], in *Gottes Offenbarung: Gesammelte Aufsätze zum Alten Testament* (TB 19; Munich: Chr. Kaiser, 1969), 234–48 (at 236–38).

commandment of the Decalogue, which prohibits the worship of other deities, in the plural: "You shall have no other *gods* before me" (Exod 20:3). Most likely, verse 5 would originally have continued directly after verse 3. At a later stage in the history of Israelite religion, as monotheism replaced monolatry, the recognition here of the existence of deities other than Yahweh became problematic or was no longer understood. It was "corrected" by means of the insertion of verse 4 to refer instead to the worship of inert idols. Later Jewish tradition implicitly recognized the problem raised by the unambiguous reference to "other gods" in verse 3, and solved the problem by means of harmonistic exegesis.[48]

The original formulation of the second commandment then continues, as God offers the following rationale for the prohibition of the worship of other deities:

> For I, Yahweh your God, am an impassioned God, *visiting the iniquity of the fathers upon the children* (פקד עון אבת על בנים), upon the third and the fourth generation *of those who reject me* (לשנאי), but showing kindness to the thousandth generation *of those who love me* (לאהבי) and *keep my commandments* (ולשמרי מצותי). (Exod 20:5–6)

The Hebrew participles translated as "those who love" and "those who reject" are not affective but legal terms. Reflecting the terminology of Hittite, Neo-Assyrian, and Aramaic

[48] The Tannaitic midrash to Exod 20:3 asks why God in the Decalogue speaks of "*other* gods" when, properly, "they were not gods" (Isa 37:19). In light of Isaiah's later polemic, the Hebrew wording is then cleverly reinterpreted as referring to "Merely those which *others* called gods." See Jacob Z. Lauterbach, *Mekilta de-Rabbi Ishmael* (3 vols.; Philadelphia: Jewish Publication Society, 1933), 2:239 (emphasis added).

state treaties, *love* designates political loyalty to the suzerain, whereas *reject* denotes acts of treason.[49] Israelite authors took over this secular treaty terminology, together with the concept of a binding legal tie, to conceptualize the nation's relationship with its God as a covenant. (Despite the narrative's ancient setting at the beginning of the nation's history, the key theological idea of the covenant actually represents a late development, which was then read back into Israel's origins.[50]) The importance of the Near Eastern treaty model for covenantal theology has long been recognized.[51] These ancient Near Eastern treaties were understood as being made in perpetuity. They were therefore binding not only upon those immediately

[49] William L. Moran, "The Ancient Near Eastern Background of the Love of God in Deuteronomy," *CBQ* 25 (1963): 77–87; reprinted in idem, *The Most Magic Word: Essays on Babylonian and Biblical Literature* (ed. Ronald S. Hendel; CBQMS 35; Washington, D.C.: Catholic Biblical Association, 2002), 170–81. See also Moshe Weinfeld, *Deuteronomy and the Deuteronomic School* (Oxford: Clarendon, 1972; reprint, Winona Lake, Ind.: Eisenbrauns, 1992), 81–91; and Udo Rüterswörden, "Die Liebe zu Gott im Deuteronomium," in *Die deuteronomistischen Geschichtswerke: Redaktions- und religionsgeschichtliche Perspektiven zur 'Deuteronomismus'-Diskussion in Tora und Vorderen Propheten* (ed. Markus Witte et al.; BZAW 365; Berlin: Walter de Gruyter, 2006), 229–38.

[50] See Lothar Perlitt, *Bundestheologie im Alten Testament* (WMANT 36; Neukirchen Vluyn: Neukirchener Verlag, 1969). For an attempt, in part, to rehabilitate and rethink the covenant in light of the theological issues raised by Perlitt's dating, see Ernest W. Nicholson, *God and His People: Covenant and Theology in the Old Testament* (Oxford: Clarendon Press, 1986). See also Eckart Otto, "Die Ursprünge der Bundestheologie im Alten Testament und im Alten Orient," *ZABR* 4 (1998): 1–84. For a recent overview of the issues, see *Covenant as Context: Essays in Honor of E. W. Nicholson* (ed. A. D. H. Mayes and R. B. Salters; Oxford: Oxford University Press, 2003).

[51] For a useful overview, see Delbert R. Hillers, *Covenant: The History of a Biblical Idea* (Baltimore: Johns Hopkins Press, 1969).

signatory to them but also upon succeeding generations. Consequently, the punishment for noncompliance stipulated the execution both of those actually party to the treaty and of their progeny. That principle of distributive justice underlies Yahweh's threat that he will visit his rage upon the third and fourth generations of those guilty of breaking the covenant.[52] The extension of retribution across three generations strikingly resembles a similar formulation found in a group of treaties made between the Neo-Assyrian ruler Esarhaddon and his eastern vassals in 672 B.C.E. To ensure their allegiance to Assurbanipal, his heir designate, Esarhaddon required that they take an oath stipulating both loyalty and accountability across three generations:

As long as *we, our sons* [*and*] *our grandsons live* (*anēnu mar'ēni mar'ē mar'ēni*), Assurbanipal, the great crown prince designate, shall be our king and our lord. If we place any other king or prince over *us, our sons, or our grandsons* (*ina muḫḫīni mar'ēni mar'ē mar'ēni*), may all the gods mentioned by name [in this treaty] hold *us, our seed, and our seed's seed* (*ina qātēni zar'*[*īn*]*i zar'i zar'īni*) to account.[53]

52 Note the thorough study by Meir Weiss, "Some Problems in the Biblical Doctrine of Retribution," *Tarbiz* 31 (1961–1962): 236–63; 32 (1962–1963): 1–18 (Hebrew); reprinted in *Likkutei Tarbiz: A Biblical Studies Reader* (ed. Moshe Weinfeld; Jerusalem: Magnes, 1979), 71–98, 99–116 (Hebrew). His argument, however, that "third and fourth" simply means "a large number of generations," and is thus equivalent to "the thousandth generation," is harmonistic. Moreover, it does not take into account the following parallels to the Neo-Assyrian treaties.

53 The translation of the Akkadian is my own. See the excellent edition by Simo Parpola and Kazuko Watanabe, eds., *Neo-Assyrian Treaties and Loyalty Oaths* (SAA 2; Helsinki: Helsinki University Press, 1988), 50 (Esarhaddon's Succession Treaty, § 57, lines 507–12); and Kazuko Watanabe, *Die adê-Vereidigung anlässlich der Thronfolgeregelung*

By transferring this Near Eastern convention from the political to the theological domain, the biblical text formulates a doctrine of the transgenerational consequences of sin: although it is my parent who wrongs God, I and my children and my grandchildren are punished for the parent's wrongdoing, independent of any particular malfeasance on our part.[54] The text is remarkably silent about whether the actual sinner is punished for his or her own offense or whether the expected punishment might be completely displaced onto the progeny.[55] Precisely this anomaly of justice occurs when God remits the capital punishment due David in double measure—for adultery with Bathsheba and for contriving the murder of Uriah,

---

Asarhaddons (BaghMB 3; Berlin: Gebr. Mann, 1987), 166–67 (with normalization). Note the similar generational reference at § 25, lines 283–91.

54 Contra Josef Scharbert, who without philological justification restricts the meaning of the key verb פקד to "test" and thereby evades the problem of theodicy; see Josef Scharbert, "Das Verbum PQD in der Theologie des Alten Testaments," *BZ* 4 (1960): 209–26 (at 219). Similarly problematic is the approach of Adrian Schenker, whose rendering corresponds nearly verbatim—though apparently unintentionally—to the postbiblical exegetical harmonization witnessed by Targum Onqelos (see "The Interpretation of Divine Justice in the Targum" in chapter 4 of this book). His reconstruction of the verse's original meaning is colored by the legal harmonizations (*midrash halakah*) evident in rabbinic eisegesis. See idem, *Versöhnung und Widerstand: Bibeltheologische Untersuchung zum Strafen Gottes und der Menschen, besonders im Lichte von Exodus 21–22* (SBS 139; Stuttgart: Katholisches Bibelwerk, 1990), 85n156 and 87.

55 Arguing that the delay in exacting punishment was intended as an expression of divine mercy toward the penitent wrongdoer, see Yochanan Muffs, *Love & Joy: Law, Language and Religion in Ancient Israel* (New York: Jewish Theological Seminary of America, 1992), 19 (on Exod 32:34). His hypothesis, however, begs the question of whether in each case the sinner is in fact penitent and deserving of such divine mercy. In that way, his argument becomes circular.

her Hittite husband—and transfers it instead to their innocent newborn son, who is stricken with a fatal illness (2 Sam 12:1–15; similarly, 1 Kgs 21:29).

Here, there emerges a fundamental ethical and theological problem: Is it not odious for God to punish innocent persons, merely for being the progeny of sinners? Abraham took God to task for just this breach of justice while bargaining over the lives of the inhabitants of Sodom: "Shall you sweep away the innocent along with the guilty? . . . Shall not the judge of all the earth deal justly?" (Gen 18:23, 25). Israelite authors keenly felt this problem of theodicy raised by the Decalogue's doctrine of transgenerational punishment.[56] It was no merely abstract or

[56] André Wénin denies that there is any problem of theodicy raised by the Decalogue's formula of transgenerational punishment in his review article, "'Dieu qui visite la faute des pères sur les fils' (Ex 20,5): En marge d'un livre récent de B. M. Levinson," *RTL* 38 (2007): 67–77. He maintains that Exod 20:5 should be translated: "Dieu . . . vient voir que la faute des pères a des conséquences sur les fils pour plusieurs generations" (70) [God . . . comes to see whether the wrongdoing of the fathers bears consequences for the sons for multiple generations]. For Wénin, it is not a case of punishing those who are potentially innocent but of mere historical investigation of whether they merit punishment. It is difficult to know how to respond to this proposal because it seems as if the main point is really a theological conviction that attempts to anchor itself in a philological argument. Although I welcome this scholar's principled challenge, I do not find myself persuaded and will attempt to respond to both dimensions of his position. As regards the philology: while claiming to provide a more precise rendering of the Hebrew verb פקד, the author overlooks the just-cited earlier work of both Scharbert ("Das Verbum PQD") and Schenker (*Versöhnung und Widerstand*), whose proposals he comes close to replicating. His recommended translation bears little relation to the grammar and syntax of the Hebrew. It divorces עוֹן אבת, "(the) iniquity of (the) fathers," from serving as the direct object of the verb פקד, "to visit," and instead shunts it into a conditional clause for which there is no evidence in the Hebrew (*whether* the wrongdoing of the fathers *bears*

modern theological problem but had vital implications for the nation's history. Ancient Israel endured a catastrophe in 587 B.C.E. when, following a two-year siege, the Babylonian army breached the walls of Jerusalem, burned the city, gutted the Temple, and deported the majority of the population to Babylon. The editor of the book of Kings, charged with narrating that history, explains the destruction as the result of divine punishment for the unprecedented iniquities committed not by the generation contemporary with the destruction but rather by King Manasseh (696–641 B.C.E.), who ruled three generations beforehand (2 Kgs 21:1–15; 23:26–27; 24:3–4; contrast 24:19–20).[57] The biblical editor had little choice: how else to explain the gutting and burning of Jerusalem that followed so shortly after the reign of righteous King Josiah, who had been heralded for his perfect devotion to the law of Moses (2 Kgs 23:25)?

---

consequences for the sons for multiple generations). The verb, when combined with a personal reference as definite direct object, may indeed mean "to visit" in a neutral way: "Samson came to visit his wife," ויפקד שמשון את אשתו (Judg 15:1). However, when the same verb instead takes a noun with the semantic range of wrongdoing or sin as its direct object, the meaning is quite different: יזכור עונם יפקוד חטאותם, "He will remember their iniquity, / He will punish their sins" (Hos 9:9; NJPS). That is the semantic construction at issue in the Decalogue's formula for transgenerational punishment. Then there is the theological issue, which is perhaps the real point of departure. In Wénin's view, the God of the Decalogue never really gets angry. He lacks the wrath to punish anyone except those who are actually guilty of wrongdoing. Although this kind of polite restraint may result in a politically correct God, in my view such a deity is consistent neither with the God of ancient Israel nor with the text of Exod 20:5.

57 There were three generations from Manasseh's reign to the time that the Babylonians ended Egyptian control over Judah and made King Jehoiakim their vassal (2 Kgs 24:1–5): Amon, Josiah, and Josiah's two sons, Jehoahaz and Eliakim/Jehoiakim. The first deportation occurred in the next (fourth) generation with the deportation of King Jehoiachin (2 Kgs 24:8–17).

4

The Reworking of the Principle of Transgenerational Punishment: Four Case Studies

CRITICAL SCRUTINY OF THE PRINCIPLE IN LAMENTATIONS

The idea of using the formula for transgenerational punishment to account for the Babylonian exile may well have become commonplace right from the beginning of the exilic period. Fugitives who fled Jerusalem seem to have inscribed key elements of the formula on the walls of caves in which they took shelter.[1] It is also reflected in a series

[1] Inscription B from the tomb cave at Khirbet Beit Lei (sixth century B.C.E.) reuses the attributes of mercy (Exod 34:6–7, which includes the transgenerational formula) in the context of a petition to be spared from punishment. See Frank Moore Cross Jr., "The Cave Inscriptions from Ḫirbat Bayt Layy [Khirbet Beit Lei]," in *Near Eastern Archaeology in the Twentieth Century: Essays in Honor of Nelson Glueck* (ed. James A. Sanders; Garden City, N.Y.: Doubleday, 1970), 299–306; reprinted in idem, *Leaves From an Epigrapher's Notebook: Collected Papers in Hebrew and West Semitic Palaeography and Epigraphy* (HSS 51; Winona Lake, Ind.: Eisenbrauns, 2003), 166–70. Arguing that the inscription represents a creative transformation of the divine attribute formula (as reflected in Exod 34:6–7) is Patrick D. Miller Jr., "Psalms and Inscriptions," in *Congress Volume, Vienna, 1980* (ed. J. A. Emerton; VTSup 32; Leiden: E. J. Brill, 1981), 311–32 (at 328–31); reprinted in idem, *Israelite Religion and Biblical Theology:*

of exilic and postexilic biblical texts. These texts confirm, however, that this historiographical "solution" created as many theological difficulties as it sought to solve. Lamentations, for example, preserves a moving poetic dirge over the destruction of Jerusalem and the suffering of its population. Near the book's close, the speaker seems to share the orientation of the historiographer of Kings as he, too, accounts for the destruction as divine punishment for the apostasy of previous generations. That rationalization is now, however, subjected to critical scrutiny.

Our fathers (אבתינו) sinned and are no more;[2]
But as for us—*the punishment for their iniquities* (עונתיהם)—we must bear! (Lam 5:7)

The terminology of the lament, which pointedly refers both to "fathers" (אבות) and to "punishment for iniquities" (עונות), alludes to the Decalogue's doctrine of the transgenerational consequences of sin, in which God describes himself as "visiting the *punishment for the iniquity* of the *fathers* upon the sons," פקד עון אבת על בנים (Exod 20:5).[3]

Collected Essays (JSOTSup 267; Sheffield: Sheffield Academic Press, 2001), 210–32. See the fresh evaluation of the evidence by Ruth Scoralick, *Gottes Güte und Gottes Zorn: Die Gottesprädikationen in Exodus 34,6f und ihre intertextuellen Beziehungen zum Zwölfprophetenbuch* (HBS 33; Freiburg: Herder, 2002), 58–60.

[2] Following the *Qere* of the MT.

[3] Providing valuable criteria to distinguish textual dependence from simple sharing of common language, and thus distinguishing between allusion (as intentional reuse) and intertextuality (which technically considers the questions of intention and of dependence irrelevant), see Benjamin D. Sommer, "Exegesis, Allusion and Intertextuality in the Hebrew Bible: A Response to Lyle Eslinger," *VT* 46 (1996): 479–89; and idem, *A Prophet Reads Scripture: Allusion in Isaiah 40–66* (Stanford, Calif.: Stanford University Press, 1998), 6–72.

The speaker has broken apart the original genitive phrase ("iniquity of the fathers") of the Decalogue, making each of its two key terms into the subject of an independent statement. As a result, God's threat of punishment is here invoked as accomplished fact—but now from the perspective of the progeny who proclaim their innocence by restricting culpability to the previous generation. By insinuating the innocence of his own generation, the speaker asserts the injustice of divine justice. Moreover, in the Hebrew of the lament, the words for "fathers" (אבות) and for "the punishment for iniquities" (עונות) are strongly linked by both assonance and rhyme. But the pronominal suffixes that specify "*our* fathers" (אבתינו) and "the punishment for *their* iniquities" (עונתיהם) break the similarity of sound. The broken assonance highlights the fractured logic: the punishment that the speakers endure is not for their own but for their *fathers'* apostasy. The indirect intertextual reference in fact amounts to the censure of a text whose infrangible authority is precisely the problem.

The injustice of the doctrine raises important practical difficulties as well. It inevitably creates an overwhelming sense of the futility of historical action altogether, inasmuch as the progeny cannot free themselves from the consequences of the past. In the grim circumstances of Israel after the catastrophe of destruction and exile, the future would have seemed radically foreclosed, the direct result not of one's own but of a previous generation's action. Yahweh himself anticipates the despair of the first group of deportees (those who had been deported with Jehoiachin in 597 B.C.E.), citing their complaint in advance: "How then shall we survive?" (Ezek 33:10) Any step forward—whether toward personal renewal or national reconstruction—would appear pointless. For both theological and existential-historical reasons, therefore, we can expect biblical authors to struggle relentlessly against the injustice of the Decalogue's doctrine.[4]

THE TRANSFORMATION OF DIVINE JUSTICE IN EZEKIEL

Precisely as Judah faced the prospect of national destruction, the prophet Ezekiel (active 593–573 B.C.E.) provided a profound meditation on the impact of temporality on human action. Ezekiel had been among the upper echelon of Judean society deported to Babylon in 597 (thus prior to the destruction of Jerusalem with its Temple, and the exile of the city's population in 587). He here reported to his fellow deportees, who lived in a period of uncertainty, still hoping for their restoration to Jerusalem, about an oracle he had recently received:

The word of Yahweh came to me: "How dare you bandy about this proverb upon the soil of Israel, '*Fathers* (אבות) eat sour grapes and their *children's* (הבנים) teeth are set on edge?' As I live—declares the Lord Yahweh—this proverb shall no longer be current among you in Israel. Consider:

[4] See Michael Fishbane, "Torah and Tradition," in *Tradition and Theology in the Old Testament* (ed. Douglas A. Knight; Philadelphia: Fortress Press, 1977), 275–82; and idem, *Biblical Interpretation in Ancient Israel* (2d ed.; Oxford: Clarendon, 1988), 335–50. The following analysis is indebted to Fishbane's work.

all lives are mine. The life of the father and the life of the child are both mine. The person who sins, only he shall die!" (Ezek 18:1–4)[5]

The proverb cited by the prophet graphically portrays transgenerational punishment. As the prophet's refutation implies, the proverb is not concerned with literal sour grapes but with moral ones, with sin and its consequences. The prophet rejects this proverb and substitutes for it a clear statement of individual responsibility: henceforth the father shall suffer for his own misdeeds; the child will be spared inherited punishment. Strikingly, while rejecting the proverb as offensive, the prophet never disputes that the moral economy it depicts has hitherto been valid. The oracle has a parallel text in Jeremiah that also rejects the proverb: "In those [future] days, no longer shall they say, 'Fathers eat unripe grapes and the teeth of the sons are set on edge,' but rather, 'Each shall die for his own iniquity; whoever eats unripe grapes, [only that person's] teeth shall be set on edge'" (Jer 31:29–30).[6] In Jeremiah's version of the oracle, the principle of individual responsibility will take effect only with the advent of a new moral and religious economy, sometime in an unspecified future (Jer 31:27, 31, 33). Jeremiah thus concedes that the proverb continues to be valid for the present and immediate future. Only in the

[5] This translation is indebted to *Tanakh: The Holy Scriptures* (Philadelphia: Jewish Publication Society, 1988); and Moshe Greenberg, *Ezekiel 1–20* (AB 22; Garden City, N.Y.: Doubleday, 1983), 325.

[6] See Christoph Levin, *Die Verheißung des neuen Bundes: in ihrem theologiegeschichtlichen Zusammenhang ausgelegt* (FRLANT 137; Göttingen: Vandenhoeck & Ruprecht, 1985), 38–39.

case of Ezekiel is the new principle immediately to replace the rejected one.

The correspondence between the rejected proverb and the doctrine of transgenerational punishment can hardly be accidental. The repudiated proverb and the Decalogue doctrine share not only the notion of retribution vicariously transmitted from one generation to the next but also common terminology: the resonant language of fathers (אבות) and children (בנים, lit., "sons"). At the same time, the overlap is only partial: sufficient for the proverb to resonate with the Decalogue doctrine, but insufficiently specific or extensive to point to an explicit citation or reuse of that text. Might Ezekiel's indirection be intentional? The proverb almost certainly functions as a straw man. The problem confronted by Ezekiel consists not simply in the popular sensibility of his time trenchantly depicted in the proverb: the perception among the exiles that they suffer innocently and that divine justice is arbitrary (see Ezek 18:25, 29; 33:17). More seriously, this popular perception of divine injustice has a foundation in ancient Israel's formative canon. The explicit rejection of transgenerational punishment would require Ezekiel to repudiate an authoritative teaching attributed to Yahweh.[7] Nevertheless,

[7] Joel S. Kaminsky regards the principle of individual responsibility advanced by Ezek 18 in ad hoc terms, as a situation-specific response, rather than as a concerted rejection of transgenerational punishment altogether, let alone as a rejection of a particular text or specific tradition (*Corporate Responsibility in the Hebrew Bible* [JSOTSup 196; Sheffield: Sheffield Academic Press, 1995], 189). While Kaminsky concedes the influence of the formula for secular justice (Deut 24:16), he denies it in the case of the formula for divine justice. His approach seeks to redress the tendency of past scholarship to impose an external agenda on the chapter by regarding it as pivotal

failure to repudiate it validates the deportees' perception that Yahweh is unjust and that their future is foreclosed.

Ezekiel therefore uses the proverb as a strategic foil for the far more theologically problematic act of effectively annulling a divine law. The prophet in effect "devoices" the doctrine's original attribution to God and then "revoices" it as folk wisdom. By this means, the oracle obscures its subversion of the divine instruction found in the Decalogue. The antithetical nature of these two texts was already recognized in the Talmud.[8] It is a much simpler matter to repudiate a folk saying than to reject the Decalogue's concept of transgenerational punishment as morally repugnant. Figure 1 shows how the formulation of the new conception of divine justice echoes the existing rule requiring individual liability in matters of civil and criminal law. In the latter sphere, biblical law prohibits vicarious punishment and specifies that only the perpetrator should be held accountable:

---

in the development of a theology of individual salvation within ancient Israel. The hesitation to assign the weight of formal doctrinal change to the chapter is therefore understandable. Yet going to the opposite extreme of denying both the diachronic development of theological ideas and the possibility of a prophetic challenge to an existing doctrine of divine justice raises an equal concern. Eliminating both possibilities denies the prophet his agency and creativity. Further, the technique used to isolate each text from the other so as to deny textual allusion or doctrinal contradiction corresponds precisely to the method of classical harmonistic legal exegesis. That approach qualifies the achievements of the otherwise-nuanced theological reading.

8 "R. Jose ben Ḥanina said: 'Our master Moses decreed four sentences against Israel, but four prophets came and annulled them (וביטלום).... Moses said, "visiting the iniquity of the fathers upon the children" [Exod 20:5b = 34:7b]. But Ezekiel came and annulled it (ביטלה): "The person who sins, only he shall die!"'" (*b. Mak.* 24a).

Fathers (אבות) shall not be put to death on account of sons (בנים), A

nor sons (ובנים) be put to death on account of fathers (אבות); B

each shall (only) be put to death for his own offense. C

(Deut 24:16)

This judicial expectation of individual retribution in the sphere of civil and criminal law almost certainly provided a means for Ezekiel to revise the standard of punishment in the sphere of theological wrongdoing. Ezekiel's formulation chiastically cites the principle of secular justice, reapplying it so that it also governs offenses against the deity:[9]

The person who sins, (only) he shall die: C′

a son (בן) shall not bear the iniquity of the father (האב), B′

nor shall a father (ואב) bear the iniquity of the son (הבן). A′

(Ezek 18:20)

Figure 1. Ezekiel's Reapplication of the Principle of Punishment in Criminal Law

The formula for individual liability in civil and criminal law thus almost certainly served as a legal and literary precedent for the prophet.[10] It enabled him or the later

[9] This analysis follows Greenberg, *Ezekiel 1–20*, 333; and Fishbane, *Biblical Interpretation*, 337–41. On inverted citation as marking reuse (as noted by Greenberg), see the analysis of Deut 7:9–10 below. The likelihood of the reuse of Deut 24:16 is increased with the recognition that Ezek 18 contains a sequence of reworking of prior legal texts (Ezek 18:7–8, 13, 16, 18 reuse Deut 23:20–21; 24:6, 10–15, 17; so Fishbane, loc. cit.).

[10] Maintaining the reverse direction of textual dependence are Levin, *Die Verheißung des neuen Bundes*, 40–43 (for whom Deut 24:16 depends on Jer 31:29) and Georg Braulik. The latter regards Deut 19–25 as a very late addition to the legal corpus that draws upon both Ezekiel and the Holiness Code (Lev 17–26). As such, he maintains that Deut 24:16 depends upon Ezek 18; see Georg Braulik, "Ezechiel

composer of this section to bring theological justice into conformity with secular justice by means of analogical legal reasoning.[11]

und Deuteronomium: Die 'Sippenhaftung' in Ezechiel 18,20 und Deuteronomium 24,16 unter Berücksichtigung von Jeremia 31,29–30 und 2 Kön 14,6," in idem, *Studien zum Deuteronomium und seiner Nachgeschichte* (SBAB 33; Stuttgart: Katholisches Bibelwerk, 2001), 171–201. Braulik scrupulously cites challenges to his redactional analysis (200n122), which I find convincing. See further Eckart Otto, *Das Deuteronomium: Politische Theologie und Rechtsreform in Juda und Assyrien* (BZAW 284; Berlin: De Gruyter, 1999), 296–98.

[11] The formulation "or the later composer of this section" is admittedly inelegant. In speaking of *Ezekiel*, I mean to designate the literary persona represented in chapter 18 and do not mean to imply that the entire chapter represents a unified literary composition that derives from the historical prophet. The compositional history of the book of Ezekiel is too complex to be addressed properly here. Two main alternatives can be mentioned. Moshe Greenberg takes a "holistic" approach that sees the book as representing a single authorial intentionality which he associates with the historical prophet (*Ezekiel 1–20*, 12–27). Most scholars, however, regard the book as having a much longer compositional history and identify literary tensions representing separate redactional layers. This approach would see the prophet as playing a much narrower role in the formation of the book. Karl-Friedrich Pohlmann maintains that Ezek 18:1–13 belongs to the oldest textual layer of the book; over the next century, verses 14–32 were added to address new historical and theological realities (*Ezechielstudien: Zur Redaktionsgeschichte des Buches und zur Frage nach den ältesten Texten* [BZAW 202; Berlin: Walter de Gruyter, 1992], 219–44; and idem, *Das Buch des Propheten Hesekiel [Ezechiel], Kapitel 1–19* [ATD 22.1; Göttingen: Vandenhoeck & Ruprecht, 1996], 257–76).

Some of Pohlmann's diachronic analysis seems arbitrary. He identifies a literary tension within verses 1–20 because the proverb of verse 2 mentions just two generations ("fathers" and "sons"), although three generations are discussed in the continuation: the situation of the father (vv. 5–9), the son (vv. 10–13), and the grandson (vv. 14–20). As a result of this perceived literary tension, he assigns the unit concerned with the third generation to a later literary layer. Pohlmann's analysis assumes, however, that the prophetic corpus evolves without any literary interaction with the literature of

In the rest of the chapter, Ezekiel exploits the proverb in an intricately crafted series of acute reflections upon morality to deprive the proverb of any moral validity whatsoever: neither righteousness nor sin, neither reward nor punishment, may be communicated between generations (18:10–20). Earlier scholars saw Ezekiel as here championing a religion of the individual in contrast to a collective religious identity and thereby transformed him into a proto-Protestant reformer. That approach, of course, is inconsistent with the priorities of the text. The doctrine of repentance cannot be viewed as operating only in the context of the individual: its application is simultaneously individual and national.[12]

---

the Pentateuch. This is, in its own way, a very conventional model that does not take into account the more complex realities of literary history during the exilic and postexilic periods. If one considers that the Decalogue's formula for transgenerational punishment represents an "intertext" engaged by Ezekiel 18, that inconsistency is resolved. It is very likely that the prophetic and pentateuchal corpora evolved in dialogue and debate with one another, and that there were many points of intertextual polemic between them.

[12] See the thoughtful study by Baruch J. Schwartz, "Repentance and Determinism in Ezekiel," *Proceedings of the Eleventh World Congress of Jewish Studies*, Division A, *The Bible and Its World* (ed. David Assaf; Jerusalem: World Union of Jewish Studies, 1994), 123–30. In contrast, other scholars properly stress the national reference but regard it as inconsistent with a focus also on the individual; see Paul M. Joyce, "Individual Responsibility in Ezekiel 18?" in *Studia biblica 1978: Sixth International Congress on Biblical Studies, Oxford, 3–7 April 1978* (ed. Elizabeth A. Livingstone; Sheffield: University of Sheffield, 1979), 185–96; and Gordon H. Matties, *Ezekiel 18 and the Rhetoric of Moral Discourse in the Book of Ezekiel* (SBLDS 126; Atlanta: Scholars Press, 1990), 113–58. Elsewhere, Paul M. Joyce astutely rejects the widespread assumption of an evolution within ancient Israel from belief in corporate responsibility to individual responsibility; see idem, "Ezekiel and Individual Responsibility," in *Ezekiel and His Book* (ed. Johan Lust; BETL 74; Leuven: Peeters Press, 1986), 317–32.

The prophet finally rejects the generational logic of the proverb altogether and transforms it into a metaphor for the freedom of an individual to transform and renew his life, at every moment in his life, whatever the burden of his past (18:21–29). Even if one has committed unremitting evil, Ezekiel contends, should one repent, one will not suffer the consequences of that evil (18:21–23, 27–29). The individual is held accountable exclusively for the moral decisions he makes in the present. Ezekiel's theology of freedom works to counter notions among his contemporaries of the futility of action. The prophet argues that the future is not hermetically closed but hermeneutically open. Ezekiel begins with inexorable fate but ends with freedom, moral action, and repentance as the sole forces that govern human action. Remarkably, that shift occurs without any explicit rejection of divine law.

Although widely heralded in standard Old Testament theologies for its focus upon the individual, Ezekiel's formulation of freedom represents a largely unrecognized landmark in the history of thought. Despite its religious terminology, it is essentially modern in its conceptual structure. With its powerful critical engagement with existing assumptions, it amounts to a theory of human action that rejects determinism, affirms individual responsibility for one's standing in the present, and mandates the importance of moral choice. Within the history of philosophy, the comparable groundbreaking conceptualization of moral freedom as independence from the burden of the past is associated with the early-modern philosopher Immanuel Kant (1724–1804). Much as Ezekiel did, Kant mounts a penetrating critique of the idea that the past determines one's actions in the present. He challenges any position that would reduce a person to his or her past and preclude the exercise of free will or the possibility of change. He maintains that persons are free at every moment to make new moral choices. His conception of freedom is dialectical: although within nature there is no freedom from causality (from an immediately preceding cause), freedom of choice exists for humans from the vantage point of ethics and religion. Kant intricately probes the issues involved in holding someone morally accountable who is a habitual liar:

> Reason is present in all the actions of men at all times and under all circumstances, and is always the same; but it is not itself in time, and does not fall into any new state in which it was not before. . . . When we say that in spite of his whole previous course of life the agent could have refrained from lying, this only means that the act is under the immediate power of reason, and that reason in its causality is not subject to any conditions of appearance or of time.[13]

[13] Immanuel Kant, *Critique of Pure Reason* (trans. Norman Kemp Smith; unabridged ed.; New York: St. Martin's; Toronto: Macmillan, 1965), 478. The original German (*Kritik der reinen Vernunft, 2. Auflage 1787*, vol. 3 of *Kants Werke: Akademie-Textausgabe; Unveränderter photomechanischer Abdruck des Textes der von der Preußischen Akademie der Wissenschaften 1902 begonnen Ausgabe von Kants gesammelten Schriften* [Berlin: Walter de Gruyter, 1968], 376) reads:

> Sie, die Vernunft, ist allen Handlungen des Menschen in allen Zeitumständen gegenwärtig und einerlei, selbst aber ist sie nicht in der Zeit, und gerät etwa in einen neuen Zustand, darin sie vorher nicht war. . . . [W]enn wir sagen, daß unerachtet seines ganzen, bis dahin geführten, Lebenswandels, der Täter die Lüge doch hätte unterlassen können, so bedeutet dieses nur, daß sie unmittelbar unter der Macht der Vernunft stehe, und die Vernunft in ihrer Kausalität keinen Bedingungen der Erscheinung und des Zeitlaufs unterworfen ist . . . (B584)

Kant here seeks to push back against contemporary philosophical doctrines of determinism: both the psychological determinism associated with Thomas Hobbes (1588–1679) and the metaphysical determinism associated with the later reception of Spinoza's thought ("Spinozism"),[14] and especially with Gottfried Leibniz (1646–1716). In contrast to such positions, he works to develop a theory of human action that justifies freedom of choice and provides human responsibility with a sound philosophical foundation. He frees the individual, at the moment of choice, in much the same way that Ezekiel did: by conceptualizing each moment in time as independent of the one that preceded it, as if it were a new beginning. He argues that the voice of reason—the possibility to make a free and moral decision—is always present to the person. Kant rejects determinism with this argument that the moral

[14] There is an intentional distinction made here between Baruch de Spinoza (1632–1677), the thinker, and Spinozism as the set of doctrines that later came to be associated with his name, including both pantheism and determinism. Examining one such current, see Yitzhak Y. Melamed, "Solomon Maimon and the Rise of Spinozism in German Idealism," *Journal of the History of Philosophy* 42 (2004): 67–96. Much more to the point is to recognize that Spinoza has widely been misread within the history of philosophy as well as within academic Jewish studies. For an invaluable corrective, integrating both the *Tractatus Theologico-Politicus* (1670) and the *Ethics* (1677), see Brayton Polka, *Between Philosophy and Religion: Spinoza, the Bible, and Modernity*, vol. 1: *Hermeneutics and Ontology*, and vol. 2: *Politics and Ethics* (Lanham, Md.: Lexington, 2006–2007). See also Nancy K. Levene, *Spinoza's Revelation: Religion, Democracy, and Reason* (Cambridge: Cambridge University Press, 2004). On the fragmentation of his thought within biblical scholarship, see my study, "'The Right Chorale': From the Poetics of Biblical Narrative to the Hermeneutics of the Hebrew Bible," in idem, "*The Right Chorale*"*: Studies in Biblical Law and Interpretation* (FAT 54; Tübingen: Mohr Siebeck, 2008), 7–39 (at 11–14).

agent is always, at each moment of choice, independent of the weight of his or her past. As Ezekiel sought to provide his community with a concept of agency, so Kant intensifies and strengthens the individual's responsibility for his or her own actions in the present.

Elsewhere Kant struggles with the implications of his position as he attempts to bring his own radical conception of moral freedom into conjunction with his philosophy of religion. If a criminal or a wrongdoer repents or "converts," does that mean he is entirely absolved of the consequences of his actions and that they simply disappear?[15] Kant is not quite as willing as Ezekiel is to wipe the slate clean and offer absolution. Yet Kant's own answer, while rhetorically always strong, seems to me to fudge on this point. He seeks to have it both ways: both freedom and the moral law, both the possibility of making a new beginning and retaining moral accountability. He recycles Pauline platitudes (the individual "dies to his old self") because he scrupulously sees the problem but is unable to provide a cogent solution. The concept of conversion or repentance is indeed a philosophical conundrum. But

[15] Immanuel Kant, *Religion within the Boundaries of Mere Reason* (1793), trans. George di Giovanni, in Immanuel Kant, *Religion and Rational Theology* (trans. and ed. Allen W. Wood and George di Giovanni; The Cambridge Edition of the Works of Immanuel Kant; Cambridge: Cambridge University Press, 1996), 39–215 (at 112–16). For the German original, see Immanuel Kant, *Die Religion innerhalb der Grenzen der bloßen Vernunft*, in vol. 6 of *Kants Werke: Akademie-Textausgabe; Unveränderter photomechanischer Abdruck des Textes der von der Preußischen Akademie der Wissenschaften 1902 begonnen Ausgabe von Kants gesammelten Schriften* (Berlin: Walter de Gruyter, 1968), 1–202 (at 72–78).

then again, it is not so clear that Ezekiel ever intended his position to represent a general amnesty for civil and criminal wrongdoing, as opposed to theological sin. The complexity of the issues is already there in the biblical text, even if not articulated in propositional language.

The question in all this, of course, is: Why does Ezekiel remain invisible to the history of philosophy? Or to put the question more pointedly, how is it that, on no less of an issue than the history of the idea of human freedom, philosophy seems to have a blind spot about its own intellectual history, about the extent to which Athens may be tied more closely to Jerusalem than anticipated, about the difficulty of drawing too easy a separation between sacred and secular, between reason and revelation? Both Ezekiel and Kant saw the complexity of the problem of moral freedom, and sought to create new possibilities of human action by rethinking, challenging, and reworking existing doctrines. Although it would be difficult to claim that Kant was directly influenced by Ezekiel, Kant knew the Bible well and regularly drew upon it in his work. Unfortunately, the division of the academic disciplines, whereby the material of the Hebrew Bible is rarely taken into account by contemporary philosophers—in contrast to the much richer situation that obtained earlier, as with Hobbes and Kant himself—makes Ezekiel's accomplishment largely inaccessible, as if it were only "theological" and not also intellectual. Once that binary opposition is overcome, it becomes clear that inner-biblical exegesis is important, not only as charting the reception and reinterpretation of the biblical text but as offering new possibilities for understanding the history of the idea of moral freedom.

THE HOMILY ON DIVINE JUSTICE IN DEUTERONOMY

An even more remarkable transformation of the Decalogue doctrine can be found within the legal corpus of the Pentateuch itself. Deuteronomy presents itself as a Mosaic address to the nation of Israel, forty years after Sinai, on the eve of the nation's entry into the promised land (Deut 1:1–3). According to the editorial superscription, Moses here explicates the laws that God had earlier proclaimed (Deut 1:5) and exhorts the nation to obedience.[16] In this new literary setting, Moses, while reviewing the past, ostensibly quotes the Decalogue (Deut 5) and then preaches to the nation concerning it. Moses thus expounds upon divine justice:[17]

> Know, therefore, that only Yahweh your God is God, the steadfast God who keeps his gracious covenant to the thousandth generation of those who love him and keep his commandments, but who requites (ומשלם) those who

[16] In Deut 5:31, the divine speaker directs Moses to "teach" (using the verb למד) the people in the commandments, although they had initially requested that he merely "tell" (דבר) them what God says to him on the mountain (Deut 5:27). The narrative thereby assigns a divine mandate to the creative work of Moses in explicating the Torah. See Jean-Pierre Sonnet, *The Book within the Book: Writing in Deuteronomy* (Biblical Interpretation Series 14; Leiden: E. J. Brill, 1997), 29–32 and 37–38. In his analysis, the scribes project their own authorial activity onto the literary figure of Moses, whose activity here also receives a divine sanction. (Note that in some Hebrew printings and in NJPS, Deut 5:27, 31 appear as Deut 5:24, 28. The Hebrew tradition simply has two alternative systems of verse numbering for both Exod 20 and Deut 5.)

[17] For the most recent analysis, see Timo Veijola, *Das fünfte Buch Mose, Deuteronomium: Kapitel 1,1–16,17* (ATD 8.1; Göttingen: Vandenhoeck & Ruprecht, 2004), 206–8.

reject him (לשנאיו)—to their face (אל פניו), by destroying them. He does not delay with anyone who rejects him—to his face (אל פניו) he requites him (ישלם לו). (Deut 7:9–10)

The vocabulary of this passage makes it clear that the speaker alludes specifically to the Decalogue, which he has previously quoted (Deut 5). This reuse of the Decalogue is marked by the ancient scribal technique of inverted citation (technically, "Seidel's law").[18] Often in the Bible and postbiblical literature, an author will quote a source in inverted order, such that a text sequence A B would recur elsewhere as B′ A′. Thus, in the present case, the first person sequence of the Decalogue referencing (A) "those who reject me" (לשנאי) and (B) "those who love me and keep my commandments" ([לאהבי ולשמרי [מצותי; Deut 5:9–10 [Qere]) is inverted. It is recast in the third person: (B′) "those who love him and keep his commandments" ([לאהביו ולשמרי [מצותיו) and (A′) "those who reject him" (לשנאיו; Deut 7:9–10 [Qere]). The Mosaic speaker purports

[18] The principle of inverted citation (see also n. 9 of this chapter) is named after its discoverer: Moshe Seidel, "Parallels between Isaiah and Psalms," *Sinai* 38 (1955–56): 149–72, 229–40, 272–80, 335–55 (at 150); reprinted in idem, *Ḥiqrei Miqra* (Jerusalem: Rav Kook Institute, 1978), 1–97 (Hebrew). Seidel's claims are often insufficiently controlled by criteria for establishing the direction of dependence. More controlled uses include those of Shemaryahu Talmon, "The Textual Study of the Bible—A New Outlook," in *Qumran and the History of the Biblical Text* (ed. Frank Moore Cross and Shemaryahu Talmon; Cambridge: Harvard University Press, 1975), 321–400 (at 362–63); Pancratius C. Beentjes, "Inverted Quotations in the Bible: A Neglected Stylistic Pattern," *Bib* 63 (1982): 506–23; and Benjamin D. Sommer, *A Prophet Reads Scripture: Allusion in Isaiah 40–66* (Stanford, Calif.: Stanford University Press, 1998), 35, and 219nn11–12. On this and related editorial markers, see Bernard M. Levinson, *Deuteronomy and the Hermeneutics of Legal Innovation* (New York: Oxford University Press, 1997), 17–20.

to provide a homiletic paraphrase of the formula for divine justice in the Decalogue.[19] In fact, the homily so fundamentally transforms the original as to revoke it. The speaker strategically deletes references to the transgenerational consequences of sin and instead asserts that God now punishes the sinner "to his face." By implication divine punishment for sin is restricted to the sinner alone. In contrast to the Decalogue, the progeny, here strikingly unmentioned, are not explicitly visited with divine punishment.[20]

[19] The proposal that לשנאו / לשנאיו, "those who reject him/anyone who rejects him" (Deut 7:10), tags לשנאי, "those who reject me" (Exod 20:5 = Deut 5:9), provides indirect evidence for the originality of לשנאי within the divine attribute formula. That indirect attestation is important because some scholars argue for the greater antiquity of a different version of the formula, where the specification "those who reject me" is absent (Exod 34:6–7; Num 14:18). That approach provides no explanation for the introduction of "those who reject him" into Deut 7:10. Contra Josef Scharbert, "Formgeschichte und Exegese von Ex. 34,6 f und seiner Parallelen," *Bib* 38 (1957): 130–50 (at 145–47); Moshe Weinfeld, *Deuteronomy and the Deuteronomic School* (Oxford: Clarendon, 1972; reprint, Winona Lake, Ind.: Eisenbrauns, 1992), 318; Fishbane, *Biblical Interpretation*, 345n72; and Konrad Schmid, "Kollektivschuld? Der Gedanke übergreifender Schuldzusammenhänge im Alten Testament und im Alten Orient," *ZABR* 5 (1999): 192–222. Also contra Schmid on this point, see Scoralick, *Gottes Güte und Gottes Zorn*, 31–32.

[20] André Wénin accepts both that Deut 7:9–10 represents a chiastic citation of the Decalogue formula and that it is antithetical in its intent, yet denies that it revises the Decalogue statement, believing the two to be mutually consistent in meaning. He maintains instead that Deut 7:9–10 corrects a possible false understanding of the Decalogue, lest someone should ever possibly imagine that God in the Decalogue could espouse transgenerational punishment. It is not clear that the Decalogue was ever understood as he advocates. For this "theologically correct" analysis, see idem (and the discussion in note 56 of chap. 3), "'Dieu qui visite la faute des pères sur les fils' (Ex 20,5): En marge d'un livre récent de B. M. Levinson," *RTL* 38 (2007): 67–77.

The doctrine of individual retribution is not presented as a departure from the status quo, as in the case of Ezekiel. Instead, the new teaching is presented as consistent with the very doctrine that it rejects: as an authoritatively taught re-citation of the original theologoumenon. Figure 2 shows how the revisionist speaker of Deuteronomy marshals the lemmas of the formula for transgenerational punishment against itself. Its key terms are adroitly redeployed so as to abrogate transgenerational punishment and mandate individual retribution.

		A	who requires	ומשלם
	B		those who reject him—*to their face,*	לשנאיו *אל פניו*
X			*by destroying them.*[21]	*להאבידו*
X			*He does not delay*	*לא יאחר*
	B'		with anyone who rejects him—*to his face*	לשנאו *אל פניו*
		A'	he requites him.	ישלם לו

Figure 2. Lemmatic Reworking in Support of Doctrinal Innovation (Deut 7:10)

The chiastic pattern of the repetition frames and thus highlights Deuteronomy's ethical innovation (marked by *X*): the introduction of the notion that God "does not delay" (לא יאחר) retributive justice, that is, that punishment no longer occurs transgenerationally. That doctrinal innovation is accomplished by means of textual reformulation. As the underlining in Figure 2 shows, a key term from the originally problematic text is cited: the form of

[21] The singular pronominal suffix is employed here in the Hebrew rather than the expected plural form; see Samuel R. Driver, *A Critical and Exegetical Commentary on Deuteronomy* (3d ed.; ICC; Edinburgh: T. & T. Clark, 1902), 102.

retribution due “those who reject him” (לשנאיו), alluding to “those who reject me” (לשנאי) in the Decalogue (Exod 20:5 = Deut 5:9).[22] Once cited, however, the term receives a different continuation: the new teaching of individual responsibility (as the italicized text in Figure 2 shows).[23] The double annotation stipulates that God requites the sinner, literally, “to his face” (אל פניו).[24] An equivalent

[22] Contra Hermann Spieckermann, who reverses the direction of literary dependence; see “Barmherzig und gnädig ist der Herr,” *ZAW* 102 (1990): 1–18 (at 6–8); reprinted in idem, *Gottes Liebe zu Israel: Studien zur Theologie des Alten Testaments* (FAT 33; Tübingen: Mohr Siebeck, 2001), 3–19 (at 7–9). That reversal was also recognized by Veijola, *Das fünfte Buch Mose*, 207n509. In this case, Spieckermann’s summary of Deut 7:9–“die Gnade hat jetzt die Form des Gesetzes” [grace now has the form of law] (5n8)–is hardly immanent in the text and comes closer to Pauline antinomianism. The close ties between the formula for transgenerational punishment and the Neo-Assyrian state treaties (overlooked in Spieckermann’s analysis) call the validity of such an approach into question.

[23] The ostensible syntactical redundancy of “to their face/to his face” (italics in Figure 2) quickly resolves itself once the larger intentionality and literary coherence of this unit are recognized. The insertions into the text are the entire point of the text: they function to transform transgenerational punishment into individual responsibility. For that reason, it makes little sense to dismiss them as secondary expansions. *Contra* Reinhard Achenbach, *Israel zwischen Verheißung und Gebot: Literarkritische Untersuchungen zu Deuteronomium 5–11* (Europäische Hochschulschriften 422; Frankfurt: Peter Lang, 1991), 227; and, following him, Veijola, *Das fünfte Buch Mose*, 206 and 208.

[24] Contrary to several modern translations, the phrase cannot mean “immediately” or “instantly.” There is no evidence in the Bible for instantaneous divine retribution for wrongdoing. Thus missing the point are the translations offered by Theophile Meek (*immediately*); see “Deuteronomy,” in *The Complete Bible: An American Translation* (ed. J. M. Powis Smith et al.; Chicago: University of Chicago Press, 1939), 158–91 (at 165); and by the new Jewish Publication Society Version (“instantly”); see *Tanakh: The Holy Scriptures* (Philadelphia: Jewish Publication Society, 1988), 286. The *Tanakh* translation must derive from Arnold B. Ehrlich, *Mikra ki-Pheschuto* (3 vols.; Berlin: M.

idiom occurs elsewhere: "Haran died *during the lifetime of* (על פני) Terah, his father" (Gen 11:28a, literally, "upon the face of"). Similarly, "Eleazar and Ithamar served as priests *in the lifetime of* (על פני) their father Aaron" (Num 3:4). As the medieval commentator Rashi (1040–1105 C.E.) accurately saw, the phrase means "in his lifetime" (בחייו).[25] The

Poppelauer, 1899–1901): 1:323. The same error also shows up as *sofort* in the German *Einheitsübersetzung* and in the commentary based upon that version: "Seine Strafe tritt nun sofort ein" (Georg Braulik, *Deuteronomium 1–16, 17* [NEchtB 15; Würzburg: Echter, 1986], 65). In light of an earlier version of this analysis (Levinson, "'Du sollst nichts hinzufügen und nichts wegnehmen' [Dtn 13,1]: Rechtsreform und Hermeneutik in der Hebräischen Bibel," *ZTK* 103 [2006], 157–83 [at 176]), Prof. Braulik has graciously accepted this suggestion. He has formally recommended that the *Einheitsübersetzung* be corrected so as to conform to the proposal here (personal e-mail, March 6, 2007).

25 Rashi frequently embeds classical rabbinic exegesis, particularly *midrash halakah*, in his commentary on the Pentateuch. In this case, his annotation directly reflects the Aramaic Targum Onqelos. The latter does not strictly translate the lemma of Deut 7:10 but rather amplifies it midrashically, to argue that God "requites the good deeds *of those who reject him in their lifetime* (בחייהון), *so as to cause them to perish.*" Ironically, the correct insight into the literal meaning of the specific phrase in the lemma—the recognition that "to his face" means "in his life"—actually comes in the service of a midrashic transformation of the verse. The verse is reinterpreted to forestall the inevitable question of theodicy raised by the verse in its literal meaning. How is it that, if God truly rewards the righteous and punishes the guilty, does the experience of life suggest the contrary: that the wicked seem to prosper in the world while the righteous suffer? The midrashic solution to the problem is to extend the analysis into the afterlife. The wicked receive reward for their good deeds only in this life, whereas they are requited for their iniquity by being denied a share in the world to come. The righteous, conversely, suffer only in this life for any iniquities they may have committed, whereas they are rewarded for their good deeds with the assurance of a place in the world to come. That extension of the time span of the verse into a putative afterlife, however, completely contradicts the radical claim for divine justice within history made by Deut 7:10. These

annotations redefine divine punishment and restrict it so that it no longer extends across generations. Instead, it applies only to the guilty, "in their own person" (so, correctly, NRSV).[26] The paraphrase of the source thus

issues are overlooked in the untenable claim concerning the Targum: "The Aramaic paraphrase is a reasonable interpretation of the verse's *peshat* [literal sense]"; so, Israel Drazin, *Targum Onkelos to Deuteronomy: An English Translation of the Text with Analysis and Commentary (Based on A. Sperber's Edition)* (Hoboken, N.J.: Ktav, 1982), 115. In its rendering of Deut 7:10, Onqelos corresponds closely to the Palestinian Targumic tradition, which has a well-known proclivity for extensive haggadic expansions. See the rendering of Deut 7:10 in Michael L. Klein, *The Fragment-Targums of the Pentateuch According to their Extant Sources* (2 vols.; AnBib 76; Rome: Biblical Institute Press, 1980): 1:213; 2:171. For the social and theological context of these additions, see Avigdor Shinan, *The Aggadah in the Aramaic Targums to the Pentateuch* (2 vols.; Jerusalem: Makor, 1979): 2:301 (Hebrew). The best edition of Rashi's Commentary on the Pentateuch, citing his classical sources (here noting the correspondence with Targum Onqelos) is Charles Ber [Ḥayim Dov] Chavel, ed., *Perushe Rashi ʿal ha-Torah* (3d ed.; Jerusalem: Rav Kook Institute, 1985–1986), 532 (Hebrew). The latter, of course, does not address the exegetical issues discussed here. For the standard English translation, see Morris Rosenbaum and Abraham Maurice Silbermann, trans., *Pentateuch with Targum Onkelos, Haphtaroth, and Rashi's Commentary* (5 vols.; London: Shapiro Valentine, 1929–1934; reprint, Jerusalem: Silbermann, 1973), 5:42.

26 A member of the Spanish school of medieval rabbinic exegesis, Abraham ibn Ezra (1089–1164 C.E.), rejected Rashi's midrashic approach. Ibn Ezra recognized that the issue in Deut 7:10 is not an opposition between this world and the afterlife but between individual responsibility and vicarious punishment. He correctly, if quietly, saw that the verse contradicts the Decalogue doctrine by restricting judgment to the agent "himself" (לעצמו). See Abraham ibn Ezra, *Commentary on the Torah* (ed. A. Weiser; 3 vols.; Jerusalem: Rav Kook Institute, 1977): 3:238 (Hebrew). For the similar insight that the punishment here applies only to the sinner *selbst* (himself), see August Dillmann, *Die Bücher Numeri, Deuteronomium, und Josua* (2d ed.; Kurzgefasstes exegetisches Handbuch zum Alten Testament 13; Leipzig: Hirzel, 1886), 274. Ironically, Ibn Ezra's rendering is almost identical to that

abrogates the source, which now propounds the doctrine of individual responsibility.

In formal terms, the new dispensation represents a studied series of annotations to the original doctrine, cited almost as a scriptural lemma that requires a gloss. In substantive terms, however, far from simply elucidating the lemma, the author of the gloss subverts it. Moreover, there is no formal demarcation between the lemma and its annotation: in effect, the gloss on the lemma is not distinguished from the lemma itself. The revisionist voice of the glossator directly continues, and is equal in authority with, the divine voice of the source.

Such learned reworking of authoritative texts to make them sanction the needs of later generations, or to sanction a later interpretation of religious law as having "scriptural" warrant, is more conventionally associated with a much later stage in the history of Judaism (ca. 200 B.C.E. through 150 C.E.). It is evident in the reuse of the Bible in the Dead Sea Scrolls, the book of Jubilees, and in the exegetical midrashim of the rabbinic period, for example.[27] Classical

---

of the modern NRSV. Making allowance for the NRSV's commitment to gender-neutral language, its correct translation ("in their own person") precisely corresponds to that earlier proposed by Ibn Ezra.

[27] The literature, of course, is vast. Demonstrating continuities of exegetical technique between biblical and postbiblical reworking of texts is Michael Fishbane, "Use, Authority, and Interpretation of Mikra at Qumran," in *Mikra: Text, Translation, Reading, and Interpretation of the Hebrew Bible in Ancient Judaism and Early Christianity* (ed. Martin J. Mulder; CRINT 2.1; Assen/Maastricht: Van Gorcum; Philadelphia: Fortress, 1988), 339–77. On explicit and implicit citations in *pesher* and non-*pesher* contexts, see Reinhard G. Kratz, "Innerbiblische Exegese und Redaktionsgeschichte im Lichte empirischer Evidenz," in *Das Judentum im Zeitalter des Zweiten Tempels* (FAT 42; Tübingen: Mohr Siebeck, 2004), 126–56.

antiquity also attests a genre of scholastic commentary, formally structured as lemma and gloss.[28] Deuteronomy's transformation of the doctrine for transgenerational punishment into one that propounds individual responsibility confirms the sophisticated use of such strategies in ancient Israel.

The authors of Deuteronomy employ two techniques to present their reformulation covertly. The first is lemmatic citation and reformulation, as what purports to be mere paraphrase in fact constitutes a radical subversion of the textual authority of the Decalogue. The new doctrine of individual retribution cites the very doctrine that it replaces, yet it does so atomistically, selectively redeploying individual words as markers of tradition while breaking down their original semantic reference.[29] Reduced to a cluster of individual lemmas and then reassembled in a new context, the older doctrine becomes infused with new content. Citation here seems to function less as an acknowledgment of the authority of a source than as a means to transform that source: to reinscribe that source in a new context that, in effect, restricts and contracts

[28] See H. Gregory Snyder, *Teachers and Texts in the Ancient World: Philosophers, Jews, and Christians* (London: Routledge, 2000), 75–82.

[29] *Contra* Joachim Schaper, who reduces to a logical absurdity the premise that the tendentious "exegetical" reworking of a prestigious or authoritative text might either abrogate that text or curtail its authority ("Schriftauslegung und Schriftwerdung im alten Israel: Eine vergleichende Exegese von Ex 20.24–26 und Dtn 12.13–19," in *ZABR* 5 [1999]: 111–32). The history of interpretation requires a more dialectical model of hermeneutics. In this example, where transgenerational punishment is replaced by individual retribution, the latter doctrine finally controls the way that the former one is understood and taught, as the Targumic tradition confirms (see the next section, "The Interpretation of Divine Justice in the Targum").

its original authority.[30] The second device is pseudepigraphy, the attribution of a text to a prestigious speaker from the past.[31] The authors of Deuteronomy do not write directly in their own voices. Instead, they harness the voice of Moses to literally and metaphorically, authorize their reformulation of the Decalogue. The risk of discontinuity with tradition is thus paradoxically avoided by attributing the revision of the Decalogue doctrine to the same Mosaic speaker credited with propounding it in the first place. Equally profound transformations of ancient Israel's formative canon take place elsewhere in Deuteronomy, especially in its legal corpus (Deut 12–26).[32]

[30] For the same phenomenon in the legal corpus of Deuteronomy, see Levinson, *Deuteronomy*, 46–48.

[31] See the stimulating analysis of Morton Smith, "Pseudepigraphy in the Israelite Literary Tradition," in *Pseudepigrapha I: Pseudopythagorica, Lettres de Platon, Littérature pseudépigraphique juive* (ed. Kurt von Fritz; Entretiens sur l'antiquité classique 18; Vandoeuvres, Geneva: Fondation Hardt, 1972), 191–215 (with ensuing panel discussion, 216–27). Both techniques are attested within the Dead Sea Scrolls; see Moshe J. Bernstein, "Pseudepigraphy in the Qumran Scrolls: Categories and Functions," *Pseudepigraphic Perspectives: The Apocrypha and Pseudepigrapha in Light of the Dead Sea Scrolls, Proceedings of the International Symposium of the Orion Center, 12–14 January 1997* (ed. Esther G. Chazon and Michael E. Stone; STDJ 31; Leiden: E. J. Brill, 1999), 1–26. With respect to redressing the theological issues raised by false attribution, see David G. Meade, *Pseudonymity and Canon: An Investigation into the Relationship of Authorship and Authority in Jewish and Earliest Christian Tradition* (WUNT 39; Tübingen: J. C. B. Mohr-Siebeck, 1986). For a discussion of pseudepigraphy's importance for the authority claim of rabbinic literature, see Martin S. Jaffee, *Torah in the Mouth: Writing and Tradition in Palestinian Judaism, 200 BCE–400 CE* (New York: Oxford University Press, 2001), 23–25.

[32] For an analysis of these changes in the areas of sacrifice, the calendar, and the public administration, see Eckart Otto, "Von der Gerichtsordnung zum Verfassungsentwurf: Deuteronomische Gestaltung

This radically revisionist Mosaic speaker of Deuteronomy, despite appearances, voices the concerns of Israelite authors who were close contemporaries with Ezekiel (593–573 B.C.E.).[33] Deuteronomy is set in the distant past, prior to Israel's entry into Canaan (thus, ca. 1200 B.C.E.). Nonetheless, most scholars date the composition of its literary core to the late seventh century, since Deuteronomy's demand for cultic centralization is viewed as the trigger of Josiah's religious reform (622 B.C.E.; 2 Kgs 22–23; compare 2 Chr 34–35).[34] Material was certainly added to

---

und deuteronomistische Interpretation im 'Ämtergesetz' Dtn 16,18–18,22," in *"Wer ist wie du, HERR, unter den Göttern?" Studien zur Theologie und Religionsgeschichte Israels für Otto Kaiser* (ed. Ingo Kottsieper et al.; Göttingen: Vandenhoeck & Ruprecht, 1995), 142–55; and Levinson, *Deuteronomy.*

33 Weinfeld, *Deuteronomy*, 158–78, 244–319.

34 For a reaffirmation of the connection between Deuteronomy's centralization of the cultus and Josiah's reform, see Norbert Lohfink, "Kultzentralisation und Deuteronomium: Zu einem Buch von Eleonore Reuter," *ZABR* 1 (1995): 115–48; reprinted in idem, *Studien zum Deuteronomium und zur deuteronomistischen Literatur IV* (SBAB 31; Stuttgart: Katholisches Bibelwerk, 2000), 131–61; Konrad Schmid, "Hatte Wellhausen Recht? Das Problem der literarhistorischen Anfänge des Deuteronomismus in den Königebüchern," in *Die deuteronomistischen Geschichtswerke: Redaktions- und religionsgeschichtliche Perspektiven zur "Deuteronomismus"-Diskussion in Tora und Vorderen Propheten* (ed. Markus Witte et al.; BZAW 365; Berlin: Walter de Gruyter, 2006), 19–43 (at 33–35); and the comprehensive analysis by Nadav Naʾaman, "The King Leading Cult Reforms in his Kingdom: Josiah and Other Kings in the Ancient Near East," *ZABR* 12 (2006): 131–68. Reinhard G. Kratz disputes any original connection between Deuteronomy and Josiah's religious reform on the basis of his reconstruction of the redactional history of 2 Kgs 22–23, where he considers the account of the discovery of the book, the making of the covenant, and the report of the cultic reform all to be secondary; see idem, *Die Komposition der erzählenden Bücher des Alten Testaments: Grundwissen der Bibelkritik* (UTB 2157; Göttingen: Vandenhoeck & Ruprecht 2000), 136, 193; translated as

Deuteronomy during the exile and subsequently also in the Persian period; the instruction concerning divine justice in Deuteronomy 7 likely derives from that later activity.[35] As Deuteronomy's authors confronted the successive threats of Neo-Assyrian and then Babylonian hegemony, they fashioned a radically new vision of religion and society to enable the nation to survive. To sanction that vision, they tied it to the very traditions that were actually displaced. Moses, prophetic intermediary and textual speaker, here mediates the innovative voice of Deuteronomy's authors.

This phenomenon is not restricted to Deuteronomy. Once read closely, the Pentateuch everywhere makes it clear that it has a vital legal and intellectual history in which later authors and editors respond to, challenge, reinterpret, reconcile, expand, and harmonize the earlier layers of the legal tradition. The latest layers of the Pentateuch are replete with examples where editors actively seek to create a uniform Scripture and a coherent tradition out of such divergence.[36] As a result, hermeneutics does not belong

The Composition of the Narrative Books of the Old Testament (trans. John Bowden; London: T & T Clark, 2005), 131, 185.

35 A. D. H. Mayes, *Deuteronomy* (NCB; London: Marshall, Morgan & Scott, 1979), 181, 186. Arguing that the chapter belongs to the postexilic period instead of the exilic period is Veijola, *Das fünfte Buch Mose*, 206–8.

36 See Eckart Otto, *Theologische Ethik des Alten Testaments* (Theologische Wissenschaft 3.2; Stuttgart: Kohlhammer, 1994), 230–4; idem, "Innerbiblische Exegese im Heiligkeitsgesetz Levitikus 17–26," in *Levitikus als Buch* (ed. Heinz-Josef Fabry and Hans-Winfried Jüngling; BBB 119; Berlin: Philo, 1999), 125–96. Also see Jan Christian Gertz, *Tradition und Redaktion in der Exoduserzählung: Untersuchungen zur Endredaktion des Pentateuch* (FRLANT 186; Göttingen: Vandenhoeck & Ruprecht, 2000), 29–73; idem, "Die Stellung des kleinen geschichtlichen Credos in der Redaktionsgeschichte von

to the reception history of Scripture alone, as is generally assumed. Instead, hermeneutics played a decisive role in the very creation of Scripture.

THE INTERPRETATION OF DIVINE JUSTICE IN THE TARGUM

With the close of the scriptural canon, texts such as Ezekiel 18 and Deuteronomy 7, whose authors had earlier struggled obliquely with the authority of the Decalogue, have now themselves won authoritative status coextensive with it. Indeed, in a striking reversal of literary history, these passages now eclipse the Decalogue's doctrine of transgenerational punishment because they mediate its reception and interpretation for later communities of readers. A text from this postbiblical period offers a final strategy for the reformulation of revelation. It is included here because, in the way it presents a revision of the original version as a faithful, authoritative translation, it builds upon the literary strategies already described and also responds to the kinds of transformations that have taken place in the interpretation of the Decalogue doctrine. As Hebrew ceased being spoken by Jews under Persian and then Hellenistic rule, it was gradually replaced by either Aramaic or Greek as the lingua franca. Consequently, translations of the Bible into these new vernacular languages became necessary to serve the liturgical needs of the community.[37]

Deuteronomium und Pentateuch," in *Liebe und Gebot: Studien zum Deuteronomium—Festschrift zum 70. Geburtstag von Lothar Perlitt* (ed. Reinhard G. Kratz and Hermann Spieckermann; FRLANT 190; Göttingen: Vandenhoeck & Ruprecht, 2000), 30–45.

37 See Emanuel Tov, "The Septuagint," and Philip S. Alexander, "Jewish Aramaic Translations of Hebrew Scriptures," in *Mikra: Text, Translation, Reading, and Interpretation of the Hebrew Bible in Ancient*

The Aramaic translation that eventually became dominant in Babylonia during the talmudic period (ca. 200–640 C.E.) is called Targum Onqelos. In the main, it is simple and nonexpansive, and commonly regarded as a literal translation of the Hebrew. In translating the Decalogue, however, Onqelos makes several telling additions to the formula for the transgenerational consequences of sin:

> ...visiting the guilt of the fathers upon the *rebellious* (מרדין) children, upon the third and the fourth generation of those who reject me, *when the children continue to sin* (כד משלמין בניא למחטי) as their fathers (בתר אבהתהון).[38]

Like the "Moses" of Deuteronomy 7, the Aramaic Targum presents itself not as a reinterpretation of an older doctrine but as the original significance of the Hebrew source text. Nonetheless, by means of their additions, the postbiblical interpreters responsible for Onqelos have God restrict the punishment so that only the guilty, never the innocent, are punished. Only when sinful action is transgenerational—"when the children continue to sin as their fathers"—is the punishment fittingly transgenerational as well. As such, only "rebellious" children are punished, never the innocent progeny of sinful fathers. The Palestinian Targums to the Pentateuch (the Fragment Targum, Neophyti 1, and Pseudo-Jonathan) attest similar revisions of the source

---

Judaism and Early Christianity (ed. Martin J. Mulder; CRINT 2.1; Assen/Maastricht: Van Gorcum; Philadelphia: Fortress, 1988), 161–88, 217–54. On the Targums, see also John W. Bowker, *The Targums and Rabbinic Literature: An Introduction to Jewish Interpretations of Scripture* (London: Cambridge University Press, 1969).

38 *Tg. Onq.* Exod 20:5; see Alexander Sperber, *The Bible in Aramaic Based on Old Manuscripts and Printed Texts*, vol. 1: *The Pentateuch according to Targum Onkelos* (Leiden: E. J. Brill, 1959; reprint, 3 vols. in 1; 3d ed.; Leiden: E. J. Brill, 2004), 122 (my translation).

text. In fact they attest an additional expansion designed to ensure the consistency of divine justice: " . . . visiting the guilt of the *sinful* fathers . . . "[39]

This radical reformulation of the original doctrine amounts to a postbiblical theodicy: the Targum's authors expunge the slightest chance of God's espousing a doctrine of injustice. What the text means, the Targum affirms, is that divine justice requires a notion of individual responsibility. There exists no adequate doctrine of divine justice except as the voice of Yahweh in the Decalogue is heard through and understood to be consistent with its ostensibly Mosaic rearticulation in Deuteronomy 7, as well as with Ezekiel's prophetic reformulation in his teaching on repentance. In making these texts consistent with one another, the authors of the Targum present their exegetical accommodation of the Decalogue to its various reformulations as the literal meaning and original significance of the Decalogue itself. "The Rabbis' skillful dealing with Scripture makes it evident that they were not slaves but masters of the letter."[40] The human voice of exegesis in the Targum thereby creates the divine voice of the Decalogue anew in its own image.

39 See Michael L. Klein, *The Fragment-Targums of the Pentateuch According to their Extant Sources* (2 vols.; AnBib 76; Rome: Pontifical Biblical Institute, 1980), 1:84; 2:53. Similarly, Alejandro Díez Macho, *Neophyti 1: Targum Palestinense Ms de la Biblioteca Vaticana*, vol. 2: *Éxodo: Edición príncipe, introducción y versión castellana* (Textos y Estudios 8; Madrid-Barcelona: Consejo Superior de Investigaciones Científicas, 1970), 2:129; and Ernest G. Clarke, *Targum Pseudo-Jonathan of the Pentateuch: Text and Concordance* (Hoboken, N.J.: Ktav, 1984), 91.

40 Reinhard Neudecker, "Does God Visit the Iniquity of the Fathers upon Their Children? Rabbinic Commentaries on Exod 20,5b (Deut 5,9b)," *Greg* 81 (2000): 5–24 (at 22).

In solving one problem, however, the Targum's revision creates others. If God punishes only those who commit wrongdoing in each generation, then the doctrine of the transgenerational consequences of sin has been entirely vitiated. Although the corrected version saves God from committing iniquity, it also makes the original text redundant. What is the logic for even mentioning the generations if it is only individual retribution that operates, no longer transgenerational punishment? Although there may be a hortatory function for the retention of the phrase—"the apple does not fall far from the tree"—the actual goal seems to be less to offer an admonition than to rewrite the text in such a way as to eliminate, ex post facto, any notion that the Decalogue might espouse a patently unjust doctrine. The drive to erase the contradiction between transgenerational punishment (Exod 20:5 = Deut 5:9) and individual retribution (Ezek 18; Jer 31:29–30; Deut 7:10), while at the same time preserving the integrity of the scriptural canon, means that the problematic doctrine is formally retained even as it is substantively repudiated by means of the strategic interpolation. The original doctrine has now been reduced to a lexical shell, devoid of its original content.

In effect the Targum has created a tertium quid: transgenerational punishment in the Decalogue is suddenly contingent upon whether each generation involved fails to make the repentance that would abrogate the retribution. With the new formulation, another paradox emerges. The attempt to eliminate the contradiction between the Decalogue and Ezekiel 18 has introduced a new version of the Decalogue consistent neither with the original Decalogue (in substance, since it now asserts individual retribution) nor with Ezekiel 18 (in form, since the prophetic teaching is now revoiced as divine, while Ezekiel's doctrine of repentance passes unmentioned). Nonetheless, that revisionist transformation of the Decalogue as propounding the doctrine of individual retribution became widely accepted in rabbinic theology, both in talmudic and medieval exegesis.[41] Ironically, the very drive to maintain the hermeneutical coherence of the canon has abrogated, both by addition and by subtraction, the primary requirement of that canon *not* to innovate, whether by addition or by subtraction.

[41] See *b. Ber.* 7a; *b. Sanh.* 27b; *b. Šebu.* 39a; as noted by Fishbane, *Biblical Interpretation*, 345n72.

5

The Canon as Sponsor of Innovation

Textual authority was widely challenged and actively debated in ancient Israel. Yet that debate took place in textual terms. The ingenuity that, for Jonathan Z. Smith, warrants the centrality of exegesis to the study of religion thus emerges as a form of creativity that has been insufficiently recognized by the discipline of academic Religious Studies. The evidence presented here makes it possible, moreover, to enrich Smith's theoretical model by complicating its assumption of a simple priority of foundational canon to subsequent exegesis. Already evident in the wide range of texts that much later came to be selected, anthologized, and incorporated into the canon is a technical facility with texts and with interpretation. The ineluctable connection between religious renewal and textual reworking brings into clear focus the role of the technically trained scribe as the agent of cultural change. The skilled scribe is both thinker and religious visionary; spirit becomes manifest in the scribe's revision of a text. From the perspective of ancient Israel, therefore, revelation is not prior to or external to the text; revelation is in the text and of the text.

The conceptual breakthrough is grounded in the text; the originality of thought is a consequence of engagement with the textual curriculum; and the break with tradition presents itself in terms of continuity with tradition. Ingenuity here takes the form of literary sophistication: the skill by means of which successive writers were able to conceal the conflict between their new doctrine of individual retribution and the authoritative principle of transgenerational punishment. That ingenuity required striking technical means—dodges both of voice (including devoicing, revoicing, and pseudepigraphy) and of the scribal craft (including Seidel's law and lemmatic citation and reapplication). This extensive repertoire of sleights of scribal hand suggests the difficulty of innovation in ancient Israel.

Paradoxically, such sophistication also underscores the wide-ranging possibilities of scribal creativity, as Israel's formative canon itself sponsors innovation even as it seems to proscribe it. Nor does the process cease with the canon's closure, as the Targum's reading of individual responsibility into the Decalogue demonstrates. The reworking of tradition presents itself as the original significance of tradition; the challenge to the source is read back into the source; the author renders his own voice silent by attributing that voice to the authoritative source, thereby allowing the author to emerge all the more powerfully as author, thinker, and reworker of tradition. The Torah is radically transformed by the interpretation of Torah.

Tradition itself emerges here as a hermeneutical construction, because the citation of tradition provides a means to rework tradition. Citation does not entail passive deference to the ostensibly authoritative—canonical—source but rather critical engagement with it.[1] That generalization holds true while the traditions of ancient Israel are still taking shape, as when the third-person Mosaic paraphrase of transgenerational punishment actually propounds individual retribution (Deut 7). It also holds true once the canon is closed. In a final turn of the screw, the Decalogue itself—according to the Targum—now propounds individual retribution. Through various genres and periods of rabbinic literature, the citation either of a scriptural or of an earlier rabbinic source will mark the transformation or even domination of that source.[2] Similar issues apply to the citation of the Hebrew Bible in the New Testament and at Qumran.[3]

[1] See Bernard M. Levinson, "The Hermeneutics of Tradition in Deuteronomy," in idem, *"The Right Chorale": Studies in Biblical Law and Interpretation* (FAT 54; Tübingen: Mohr Siebeck, 2008), 256–75.

[2] On midrashic citation of Scripture as involving transformation of Scripture, see Daniel Boyarin, *Intertextuality and the Reading of Midrash* (Bloomington: Indiana University Press, 1990), 35. On the Amoraic domination of the Mishnah in a *sugya* from the Palestinian Talmud, see Martin S. Jaffee, "The Pretext of Interpretation: Rabbinic Oral Torah and the Charisma of Revelation," in *God in Language* (ed. Robert P. Scharlemann and Gilbert E. M. Ogutu; New York: Paragon House, 1987), 73–89.

[3] See Joseph A. Fitzmyer's discussion of "accommodated texts" in "The Use of Explicit Old Testament Quotations in Qumran Literature and in the New Testament" [1960–61], reprinted in idem, *The Semitic Background of the New Testament* (Grand Rapids, Mich.: William B. Eerdmans; Livonia, Mich.: Dove, 1997), 3–58 (at 33–45); Elisha Qimron and John Strugnell, *Qumran Cave 4, V: Miqṣat Maʿaśe ha-Torah* (DJD 10; Oxford: Clarendon, 1994), 51, 141 (showing that the citation formula, "it is written," may refer either to a paraphrase of a text or to no known scriptural text at all); and Johan M. Lust, "Quotation Formulae and Canon in Qumran," in *Canonization and*

Israel's concept of textual authority was thus profoundly dialectical: the break with tradition validates itself in the vocables of tradition. For all the rhetoric of concealment—the impossibility of making innovation explicit or of employing the human voice—the very act of concealment, marked by the deliberate strategies just identified, reveals the innovator, the human author, at work. Notwithstanding its ostensible powerlessness before the authority of the canon, the human voice in ancient Israel was not diminished but augmented. Through its various forms of indirection, it purchased an autonomy sufficient to challenge tradition, sufficient to reject the received understanding of divine punishment and to substitute a new principle of justice. The divine speech of biblical law and prophecy reveals the transformative human voice: the voice of authors, thinkers, writers, passionately engaged with tradition.

The religious creativity of ancient Israel thus poses a challenge to the disciplinary conventions of the science of the History of Religions. It refuses any easy dichotomy between philology and phenomenology, between grammar and spirit, between technical scribal training and religious creativity. The discipline of Biblical Studies receives an equally important challenge. If the History of Religions must come to terms with "text," so, conversely, must Biblical Studies recognize "meaning" and "spirit" as animating the editorial activity that it seeks to trace in its analysis

---

Decanonization: Papers Presented to the International Conference of the Leiden Institute for the Study of Religions (LISOR), Held at Leiden, 9–10 January 1997 (ed. Arie van der Kooij and Karel van der Toorn; SHR 82; Leiden: E. J. Brill, 1998), 67–77.

of syntax and grammar. But the issues extend beyond the academic study of religion.

By challenging disciplinary conventions of both method and theory, the paradoxical structure of textual authority in ancient Israel opens out to the humanities. Except for a rather uncontrolled interest in postbiblical rabbinic midrash, which has come to be heralded as a model of textual indeterminacy and deconstructive reading, contemporary theory has all but divorced itself from the study of Scripture, from thinking in a sophisticated way about religion. The biblical text, in particular, is regarded as a parade example of an unredeemed text that encodes and perpetuates concepts of power, hierarchy, domination, privilege, xenophobia, patriarchy, and colonialism. The truth is much more complex. Unfortunately, many within the broader academic community are woefully uninformed about how to read the Bible critically, historically, and intellectually. The loss of a historical and of a philological approach to Scripture, and the divorce of contemporary literary theory from Biblical Studies and Religious Studies, has transformed the scriptural text into a golden calf, lacking in intellectual complexity, awaiting theory for its redemption.

Once viewed adequately, however, the scriptural canon itself deconstructs the false dichotomies that are repeatedly projected on to it. Theory does not bring hermeneutics or revisionist reading to the ancient text; the text invites the capable reader to recognize the theory latent in it. The canonical text arises from and sustains its own history of reception and interpretation. Although chronologically prior, the canonical source is not ontologically prior, because the past is rethought and interpreted from the vantage point of the present. The authoritative source thus reveals hermeneutics. If canonization conventionally represents an anthologizing attempt to gain closure, then the texts of the Hebrew Bible militate in the opposite direction. They resist any simple notion of canonical authority or of Scripture as one-sidedly divine. They tolerate no such hierarchies or binary oppositions. The so-called canon formula may sound like a simple, rigid commandment that inhibits renewal: "You must not add anything to what I command you nor take anything away from it." Yet from its very first appropriation by ancient Israelite authors, it already marked a site of creative textual transformation. At every point where fidelity to the canon is invoked, closer examination shows the issues to be much more complicated, with the claim of an unchanging canon itself finally emerging as an authorial construction to sanction innovation. Seen from that vantage point, the canon is radically open. It invites innovation, it demands interpretation, it challenges piety, it questions priority, it sanctifies subversion, it warrants difference, and it embeds critique. Scholars across the humanities would benefit from deeper exploration of this rich paradox.

6

The Phenomenon of Rewriting within the Hebrew Bible: A Bibliographic Essay on Inner-Biblical Exegesis in the History of Scholarship

The annotated bibliography that follows does not aim to recapitulate the titles and discussions found in the preceding chapters. Instead, the goal here is to offer a broader intellectual genealogy of the approach frequently designated "inner-biblical exegesis." That approach, I strongly believe, provides one way to trace key trends in the history of the discipline of academic Biblical Studies, from its origins in nineteenth-century European source-critical scholarship. The two approaches should not be seen as mutually exclusive; they are too frequently held apart from each other. The arrangement of entries is primarily chronological, according to the dates of the authors discussed (and not necessarily their published works). Some of the following authors have opened up a distinctive line of research (as in the case of Renée Bloch and Brevard S. Childs). In such cases, related works by other authors are grouped with them so as to show the continuity of approach, before then resuming the historical presentation. The last section of this essay, "Approaches to Exegesis in 1–2 Chronicles," departs somewhat from the preceding organizational logic;

the authors have been selected on the basis of their specific work on Chronicles.

Wellhausen, Julius. *Prologomena zur Geschichte Israels* (2d ed.; Berlin: Georg Reimer, 1883). Reprinted from the 6th ed. (1927), with an index of biblical references (Berlin: de Gruyter, 2001). English translation of the German original of 1878 by J. Sutherland Black and Allan Menzies, *Prolegomena to the History of Israel.* Preface by W. Robertson Smith. Edinburgh: Adam & Charles Black, 1885. Reprinted, with new preface by Douglas A. Knight. Scholars Press Reprints and Translation Series 17. Atlanta: Scholars Press, 1994.

Wellhausen prepared the classical, brilliantly argued model of the Documentary Hypothesis by comparing the legal collections of the Pentateuch both with one another and with the narrative works of the Deuteronomistic History (Josh, Judg, 1–2 Sam, 1–2 Kgs) and Chronicles. He began with the recognition by previous scholars that Deuteronomy's call for the restriction of all sacrificial worship of God to one exclusive sanctuary (Deut 12) ties that law corpus closely to Josiah's reform of 612 B.C.E. (2 Kgs 22–23) as the logical time of its composition. From that perspective, Deuteronomy's requirements were actually a departure from tradition and not simply a reform in which the nation returned to older norms. This conclusion suggested itself because the requirement for cultic centralization contradicted the sanction for the worship of God at multiple altar sites evident in both law (as at Exod 20:24) and narratives like Genesis 12, 1 Samuel 1, and 1 Kings 18. He therefore dated the Covenant Code prior to Deuteronomy and maintained that the priestly laws of the Holiness Code assumed centralization and therefore came after Deuteronomy, dating to the postexilic period (fifth century B.C.E.). Wellhausen's model was rooted in European Romanticism and consequently assumed the "spontaneous" religious spirit to be more creative and meaningful than one that consciously employs literary activity and the intellect. The movement to law and to text was therefore seen as a "fall": one in which the alleged creative originality becomes fossilized. This model carried with it an ill-conceived hierarchy that stigmatized cultic law and postexilic Judaism as declines from the heights of Israelite religion, which found its glory in the prophets. In fact, the extensive literary remains of the ancient Near East, already beginning to emerge as Wellhausen wrote, with their evidence for the antiquity of literacy and law, and their attention to cultic regulations, preclude such an approach.[1] Paradoxically, however, with its textual focus, Wellhausen's method comes much closer to the scribal culture of both Sumero-Akkadian literature and formative Judaism than many of the later developments within biblical scholarship for nearly a century (including that of classical form-criticism). With its scrupulous attention to how the laws and narratives of the Hebrew Bible relate to

[1] Note the powerful critique of Wellhausen by Jon D. Levenson, *The Hebrew Bible, the Old Testament, and Historical Criticism: Jews and Christians in Biblical Studies* (Louisville, Ky.: Westminster/John Knox, 1993), 10–15, 41–43. Taking a different approach, Karl Rudolf, "Wellhausen as an Arabist," *Semeia* 25 (1982): 111–55; Bernard M. Levinson, "Goethe's Analysis of Exodus 34 and Its Influence on Julius Wellhausen: The *Pfropfung* of the Documentary Hypothesis," *ZAW* 114 (2002): 212–23; Reinhard G. Kratz, *Reste hebräischen Heidentums am Beispiel der Psalmen* (Nachrichten der Akademie der Wissenschaften zu Göttingen, I. Philologisch-Historische Klasse 2; Göttingen: Vandenhoeck & Ruprecht, 2004); and Peter Machinist, "The Road Not Taken: Wellhausen and Assyriology" (in preparation).

and engage one another, his volume models a powerful way to read and understand ancient Israelite textuality.

Seeligmann, Isaac [Isac] Leo. *The Septuagint Version of Isaiah and Cognate Studies.* Edited by Robert Hanhart and Hermann Spieckermann. FAT 40. Tübingen: Mohr Siebeck, 2004.
———. *Gesammelte Studien zur Hebräischen Bibel.* Edited by Erhard Blum. FAT 41. Tübingen: Mohr Siebeck, 2004.

Seeligmann's work has just been collected and reprinted in an important German series, with significant introductions that recognize his contributions to the field. His crucial work on the Septuagint version of Isaiah (1948; reprint, 2004) already begins to provide a model of exegesis as essential to understanding the formation of the Septuagint. This approach thus breaks down any facile distinction between lower criticism and higher criticism. His works on the Hebrew Bible, gathered together in the valuable edited volume published in 2004, are crucial for the development of inner-biblical exegesis. Particularly significant are "Voraussetzung der Midraschexegese" ["The Presuppositions of Midrashic Exegesis"] (1953) and "Indications of Editorial Alteration and Adaptation in the Masoretic Text and Septuagint" (1961). The volume also includes "Anfänge der Midraschexegese in der Chronik" ["The Beginnings of Midrash in the Books of Chronicles"], a German translation of an essay published earlier in Hebrew (1979–1980), one that has been very influential and for which, unfortunately, there is not yet an English translation.

Rawidowicz, Simon. "On Interpretation." *PAAJR* 26 (1957): 83–126. Reprinted: pages 45–80 in idem, *Studies in Jewish Thought.* Foreword by Abram L. Sachar and biographical introduction by Benjamin C. I. Ravid. Philadelphia: Jewish Publication

Society, 1974. The reprint abridges the notes and deletes the extensive quotations of ancient, medieval, and early modern sources. The first publication provides these citations in the original Hebrew, Aramaic, and Latin, without English translation.

RAWIDOWICZ argues that hermeneutics should be seen as a fundamental category of Jewish intellectual history. He challenges the standard dichotomy between creation and interpretation, whereby the former category is alone regarded as an expression of originality, whereas the latter is traditionally viewed as derivative and uninspired. Interpretation does not mean simply articulating what is implicit in a textual source. Using the literature of classical rabbinic Judaism, Rawidowicz develops a much more powerful model of what he terms *interpretatio* as creatively going beyond an earlier source. He argues that the religious culture of Second Temple Judaism, with its oral Torah, was not an epigone of preexilic Israelite literature and thought but was equally creative with it. To drive this point home, he cites a late medieval midrash which insists that, in relation to earlier tradition, the rabbis did not merely drink stale water from "a cistern" (בור) but were like "a spring" (מעיין), from which fresh and living water flowed. In the dialogue, Rabbi Johanan ben Zakkai explains the contrasting metaphors to his pupil, Rabbi Eliezer ben Hyrkanos: "You are able to speak words of the Torah in excess of what Moses received at Sinai."[2]

[2] *Pirqe Rabbi Eliezer*, chapter 2, lines 2–6, my translation. This parable is cited in Hebrew by Rawidowicz, "On Interpretation," 97n28 (his reference has a typo for the chapter number). This important footnote was omitted from the reprint. Rawidowicz follows a slightly different text (שקבלת בסיני), "what you received from Sinai," rather

Rawidowicz's strong argument for the creativity of Second Temple rabbinic literature, given the pointed imagery of this midrash, seems likely to be a canny riposte to Julius Wellhausen, although the latter is never named in the essay:

Erkennt man an, daß der Kanon das Judentum vom alten Israel unterscheidet, so erkennt man auch an, daß die schriftliche Thora das Judentum vom alten Israel unterscheidet. Das Wasser, das in der Vergangenheit gequollen war, faßten die Epigonen in Cisternen. (*Prologomena zur Geschichte Israels*, 409)

[When it is recognized that *the canon* is what distinguishes Judaism from ancient Israel, it is recognized at the same time that what distinguishes Judaism from ancient Israel is *the written Torah.* The water which in old times rose from a spring, the Epigoni stored up in cisterns. (*Prolegomena to the History of Israel*, 410)]

For Wellhausen, the exile marks the transition from a living, oral tradition to textual canon and therefore from

---

than שקבל משה מסיני, "what Moses received from Sinai." There is no adequate critical edition of this fascinating ninth-century composition. An electronic critical edition remains underway by Lewis M. Barth. My Hebrew text follows the facsimile edition of C. M. Horowitz, *Pirke de Rabbi Eliezer: A Critical Edition, Codex C. M. Horowitz* (Jerusalem: Makor, 1972), 23 (incorporating the editor's handwritten corrections to the printed edition of Venice 1544). There is an English translation by Gerald Friedlander, *Pirḳê de Rabbi Eliezer (the Chapters of Eliezer the Great) according to the Text of the Manuscript Belonging to Abraham Epstein of Vienna* (London: Kegan Paul, 1916; reprinted, New York: Harmon, 1965), 6. There is a recent German edition that here overlooks the textual corrections by Horowitz although it is ostensibly based upon that facsimile edition; see Dagmar Börner-Klein, *Pirke de-Rabbi Elieser: nach der Edition Venedig 1544 unter Berücksichtigung der Edition Warschau 1852* (Studia Judaica 26; Berlin: Walter de Gruyter, 2004), xvi, 8–9.

creativity to stagnation. By situating the *spring* in the Second Temple period rather than in the preexilic period, Rawidowicz stands Wellhausen's assumption on its head. The rabbis are not *Epigoni* and canonization marks a new beginning. "Oral" creativity does not cease with the move towards textualization in the postexilic period, as Israelite religion becomes Judaism. The oral Torah, as a living tradition of interpretation, provides an ongoing form of creativity that exceeds what is given in the received written Torah.

Rawidowicz's model of postbiblical Judaism contrasts sharply with the notion of *Spätjudentum* advanced by Wellhausen and others. Taking into account that the essay was written less than a decade after the founding of the modern state of Israel in 1948 adds another important dimension to the analysis. His revalorization of the Second Temple period responds equally to the Zionist historiography of his time, which had framed the post-70 period, with its loss of political autonomy, as one of cultural desiccation and decline. In contrast, his affirmation of this period boldly sanctions Jewish life in the Diaspora as having its own cultural vitality, one not subordinate to that taking shape in the fledgling state. Rawidowicz's intellectually daring project combines philosophical sophistication with mastery of a wide range of primary and secondary sources. To advance his new model of the "Second Temple" period (*Bayith Sheni* is the term he employs), he makes two significant intellectual moves: (1) he redefines the period temporally, so that it continues long past the Roman destruction of the Temple in 70 C.E.; and (2) he expands it conceptually, so that it no longer refers to a Temple-based religion but serves as a metonym for the culture of text and interpretation more conventionally associated with the rabbinic movement of the *post*-Second Temple period. The essay thus embodies the very model of creative interpretation and revisionist rewriting that it purports only to describe. The dynamic that Rawidowicz isolates is essential to the understanding of inner-biblical exegesis.

Bloch, Renée. *Midrash.* Pages 1263–81 in *Supplément au Dictionnaire de la Bible.* Edited by Louis Pirot, André Robert, and Henri Cazelles. Book 4, suppl. 5. Paris: Librairie Letouzey et Ané, 1957.

Le Déaut, Roger. "A propos d'une définition du midrash." *Bib* 50 (1969): 395–413. Review article of Addison Wright. *The Literary Genre Midrash.* Staten Island, N.Y.: Alba House, 1967.

By drawing attention to the midrashic dimension of large sections of the biblical corpus, Renée Bloch has done pioneering work. She argues that a wide range of prophetic, poetic, and wisdom literature in the Bible should be seen as a form of rereading (the elegant French term is *relecture*) and developing earlier, more classical compositions. This approach offers an important insight into the growth of the biblical literary tradition. In this article, she also shows how fellow Francophone researchers have similarly pursued an interest in forms of inner-biblical interpretation. She properly singles out André Robert, who from 1934 onward argued for a *style anthologique* (see his "Les genres littéraires," *Supplément au Dictionnaire de la Bible* 5 [1957]: 405–21) and Albert Gélin ("La question des 'relectures' bibliques à l'intérieur d'une tradition vivante," *Sacra Pagina* 1 [1959]: 303–15). One weakness of this earlier approach, however, is that it does not yet provide methodological controls: criteria for distinguishing between literary dependence and textual reuse, on the one hand, and simple sharing of language that might be common to a given genre (such as a lament or wisdom instruction). Only in the former case—distinguished, for example, by clusters of words or phrases in a specific pattern and by matters of content—would there be proper *relecture*. Due attention to specific scribal practices and hermeneutical procedures helps consolidate these insights (see FISHBANE [1985], 286–89 and 431–33).

Another French-language pioneer is Roger LE DÉAUT, who has prepared important translations of the major Targums and is very much at home in the world of rabbinic literature. Here, in response to WRIGHT (who champions a formal definition of *midrash* as "biblical commentary"), Le Déaut emphasizes the genre's imaginative power and capacity for textual transformation. Ideally, the two polar positions should be balanced with an approach that pays careful attention to the technical and formal aspects of the genre while also recognizing its creativity.

GREENBERG, Moshe. "Some Postulates of Biblical Criminal Law." Pages 5–28 in *Yehezkel Kaufman Jubilee Volume*. Edited by Menahem Haran. Jerusalem: Magnes, 1960. Reprinted: pages 25–41 in idem, *Studies in the Bible and Jewish Thought*. JPS Scholar of Distinction Series. Philadelphia: Jewish Publication Society, 1995.

Most scholars have directed their attention to reconstructing the correct sequence and development of the biblical legal collections in relation to one another and to the narrative strands of the Bible. In comparison to that valuable literary-historical enterprise, GREENBERG's "Some Postulates of Biblical Criminal Law" (1960) remains an important attempt to articulate the meaning and significance of biblical law on its own terms. Focusing on the Covenant Code (Exod 21–23) as the earliest legal source in the Bible, he contrasts its set of values with those of the great ancient Near Eastern legal collections like the Laws of Hammurabi (1752 B.C.E.), with which it shares a great deal, both in form and in content. Two contrasting principles of sanction operate in each legal collection: either talion ("an eye for an eye") or financial compensation (a fine) may be imposed as penalties for wrongdoing. Nevertheless, within each culture, they operate differently. In the Babylonian context, talion may be imposed either for property crimes (such as theft) or for bodily injury; similarly, homicide is punishable either by financial compensation or by death, depending on the class of the victim.[3] In the biblical context, by contrast, property crime is never punishable by execution of the thief, whereas bodily injury is never compensated for in financial terms. The significance of this distinction is that the biblical legislator views "property" and "person" as separate legal and conceptual categories. Financial compensation marks property loss as finite and replaceable; talion marks the person as infinite in value and irreplaceable, which is to say, unique. The categorical distinction between the two categories is absent in cuneiform law. In this way, Greenberg demonstrates both

[3] Carrying this project forward is Pamela Barmash, *Homicide in the Biblical World* (New York: Cambridge University Press, 2005). Whereas Greenberg and Finkelstein (discussed herein) based their generalizations on analysis of the formal, literary collections of law (e.g., the Laws of Hammurabi), Barmash provides a very systematic analysis of a much broader range of sources, with particular attention to actual documents of law, including letters and trial records. She also provides an extensive analysis of the biblical material, both narrative and legal, relevant to homicide. I disagree, however, with her position that the biblical legal collections do not have literary connections to one another and lack legal development.

the ethical and the hermeneutical structure that underlies the Covenant Code.

Engaging as it is, this programmatic essay was never systematically fleshed out. There are several ways that its assumptions should be complicated. Many scholars would consider the laws of the Covenant Code not to have dispositive or statutory force but rather, on analogy with the literary collections of cuneiform law, to represent something closer to ideal reflections upon social order and ethics. In that case, it becomes much more difficult to claim that the formalized statements in either the Covenant Code or Hammurabi's Code reflect actual legal practice in their respective cultures. There are almost certainly many more continuities of legal practice "on the ground" than there are discontinuities. Indeed, there are many instances where the norms of biblical law are inconsistent with the evidence of other genres, such as narrative and wisdom, in the Hebrew Bible. For example, although biblical law prescribes death to both the adulterer and the wife as the penalty for adultery (Deut 22:22), that seems unlikely to have been implemented. Much more likely is the situation contemplated by Proverbs, where no mention is made of punishment to the wife and where the husband seeks personal physical revenge against the adulterer in a way that seems to fall short of death (Prov 6:32–35).[4]

4 Bernard S. Jackson makes this point in his sharp challenge to Greenberg's views in "Reflections on Biblical Criminal Law," in idem, *Essays in Jewish and Comparative Legal History* (SJLA 10; Leiden: E. J. Brill, 1975), 25–63. Greenberg responded to Jackson's attack in "More Reflections on Biblical Criminal Law," *Studies in Bible* (ed. Sara Japhet; ScrHier 31; Jerusalem: Magnes 1986), 1–18.

Sandmel, Samuel. "The Haggadah within Scripture." *JBL* 80 (1961): 105–22.

A New Testament scholar who transitioned to the Hebrew Bible, Sandmel suggests an original way to understand the classic problem of literary doublets and repetitions within the patriarchal narratives, such as the wife-sister motif (Gen 12:10–20, 20:1–18, 26:1–16). Traditional source criticism maintains that these repetitions derive from literary documents that were originally independent one from another. The repetitions are then used to reconstruct the separate sources of the Pentateuch according to the so-called Documentary Hypothesis. In his analysis of the motif of the Israelite matriarch in danger, Sandmel proposes a provocative alternative: the variations represent a continual process of moral and theological revision of the original narrative found in Genesis 12. Successive authors attempted to exculpate Abraham from the perception of dishonesty and moral failure (all but pimping Sarah, his wife, to Pharaoh so as to save himself) and to establish Sarah's sexual purity while she was in Pharaoh's house. These new compositions, which responded to the earlier narrative and "corrected" it, were included in the overall pentateuchal narrative because of the disinclination, Sandmel maintains, of ancient scribes to expunge objectionable material from their textual tradition. The essay inevitably raises some questions, including whether the point of departure in Genesis 12 can actually be dated as early as Sandmel assumes. Nevertheless, by turning to Second Temple literature and the model of ongoing reflection and midrashic commentary upon a text— "the Haggadah within Scripture"—Sandmel offers a stimulating way to rethink standard source-critical models.

SCHOLEM, Gershom. "Tradition und Kommentar als religiöse Kategorien im Judentum." *ErJb* 31 (1962): 19–48. Translated as "Revelation and Tradition as Religious Categories in Judaism." Pages 282–303 in idem, *The Messianic Idea in Judaism and Other Essays on Jewish Spirituality*. New York: Schocken, 1971.

SCHOLEM helped pioneer the academic study of Jewish mysticism, the literature of medieval Kabbalah. One of his major contributions in this regard is the recognition of the nature of religious tradition as a literary and intellectual construction. In this essay, which is written densely and warrants several readings, he demonstrates that tradition is not something that is simply given or immanent: it is not a passively received inheritance from the past. Instead, it should be regarded as a creative and often-arbitrary selection from that past. He shows the extent to which this takes place in each stage of Jewish literary history. As the ancient rabbis of Pharisaic Judaism present themselves as the heirs of an unbroken tradition from Sinai, so does medieval Kabbalah present itself as an ancient rabbinic tradition, just as later Lurianic Kabbalah similarly views itself as continuous with the past. At each stage of growth and transformation, the continuity with the past is asserted, and the creativity of the new religious or literary content is presented as implicit in and derived from the traditions of the past. This brilliant and dialectical analysis of the relationship between tradition and innovation has important implications for the history of interpretation. In many ways, the same model can be applied to the growth of the biblical tradition itself as it was taking shape prior to the closure of the canon.

SARNA, Nahum M. "Psalm 89: A Study in Inner Biblical Exegesis." Pages 29–46 in *Biblical and Other Studies.* Edited by Alexander Altmann. Brandeis University Studies and Texts 1. Cambridge: Harvard University Press, 1963. Reprinted: pages 377–94 in idem, *Studies in Biblical Interpretation.* JPS Scholar of Distinction Series. Philadelphia: Jewish Publication Society, 2000.

The analysis of Psalm 89 provided by SARNA recognizes the extent to which the very composition of the psalm can only be understood in exegetical terms. He demonstrates its literary dependence upon the Davidic dynastic oracle (2 Sam 7) and argues that it reinterprets its terms on account of a historical crisis. Sarna also provides an engaging introduction to the importance of texts in the ancient Near East, as the proper context for understanding Israelite authorship. Although it is possible to question the exact historical conclusions reached in this groundbreaking article, the approach it provides is invaluable.

SANDERS, James A., ed. *The Psalms Scroll of Qumrân Cave 11 (11QPs^a).* DJD 4. Oxford: Clarendon, 1965.

———. "'Adaptable for Life': The Nature and Function of Canon." Pages 531–60 in *Magnalia Dei: The Mighty Acts of God. Essays on the Bible and Archaeology in Memory of G. Ernest Wright.* Edited by Frank Moore Cross, Werner E. Lemke, and Patrick D. Miller Jr. Garden City, N.Y.: Doubleday & Co., 1976. Reprinted: pages 9–39 in SANDERS, ed., *From Sacred Story to Sacred Text: Canon as Paradigm.* Philadelphia: Fortress, 1987.

———. "Hermeneutics of Text Criticism." *Textus* 18 (1995): 1–26.

———. Review article of the *Hebrew University Bible and Biblia Hebraica Quinta. JBL* 118 (1999): 518–26.

———. "Intertextuality and Dialogue: New Approaches to the Scriptural Canon." Pages 175–90 in *Canon versus Culture: Reflections on the Current Debate.* Edited by Jan Gorak. Wellesley Studies in Critical Theory, Literary History, and Culture 23. New York: Garland, 2001.

———. *Torah and Canon.* 2d ed. Eugene, Ore.: Cascade Books, 2005.

———. Review article of David M. CARR. *Writing on the Tablet of the Heart. RBL* (2006), http://www.bookreviews.org/pdf/4703_5599.pdf; cited January 30, 2007.

McDONALD, Lee Martin, and James A. SANDERS, eds. *The Canon Debate.* Peabody, Mass.: Hendrickson, 2002.

"Surely a maggot cannot praise thee nor a grave worm recount thy loving-kindness." Early in his career, James A. SANDERS confronted this verse, which has no biblical equivalent, in "Plea for Deliverance," a noncanonical psalm found in the great Psalms Scroll (11QPs[a]), column 19, from Qumran. He had been invited to Jerusalem in 1961 to prepare the critical edition of one of the longest of the Dead Sea Scrolls, which had been discovered five years earlier (the first cache of the scrolls was discovered in 1947). The scroll immediately raised fundamental questions about the nature of the biblical text, the history of the canon, and the relative authority of various textual traditions. The Psalms scroll has a different order, content, and number of psalms than does the standard Hebrew or Masoretic text of the Bible. It provided two short psalms that seem to provide evidence of a Hebrew *Vorlage* for Psalm 151, which is extant in the Septuagint version but was previously unknown in Hebrew. The question that Sanders had to address was what was the nature of this text: had it been accepted at Qumran as part of the community's Bible—that is, was it seen as in some way authoritative?—or was it somehow simply a liturgical text, for purposes of worship only? Or was it set aside in Cave 11 as some kind of maverick text, explicitly recognized as nonbiblical? At a time when many scholars were taking decades to publish the scrolls, Sanders was able to prepare the critical edition of the text in just four years. It was published by DJD in 1965.

Sanders went on to concentrate on the formation of the biblical text and to analyze the history, function, and emergence of the scriptural canon, with particular attention to its role in creating a sense of community identity. He has made lasting contributions in both areas. As regards the first, he was part of the original team of six scholars that made up the Hebrew Old Testament Text Project (which also included Dominique Barthélemy of Fribourg, Hans Peter Rüger of Tübingen, Norbert Lohfink of Frankfurt, A. R. Hulst of Utrecht, and W. D. McHardy of Oxford). The group met for a month every summer for more than a decade to work through an extensive set of text-critical questions. The publications that resulted from that effort remain valuable as windows into the formation of the biblical text, with particular attention to the history of interpretation (including medieval Jewish grammarians) as shedding light on textual difficulties.[5] Their approach and their published findings have had an important impact upon the development of *Biblia Hebraica Quinta*, one of

[5] Dominique Barthélemy, ed., *Critique textuelle de l'Ancien Testament: Rapport final du Comité pour l'analyse de l'Ancien Testament hébreu institué par l'Alliance Biblique Universelle* (4 vols.; OBO 50; Freiburg: Universitätsverlag; Göttingen: Vandenhoeck & Ruprecht, 1982–2005); and Dominique Barthélemy et al., eds., *Preliminary and Interim Report on the Hebrew Old Testament Text Project* (5 vols.; 2d rev. ed.; New York: United Bible Societies, 1979–1980).

the two major new scholarly editions of the biblical text that is now in process (the other is the Hebrew University Bible Project). This process is described in Sanders's review of the first volume of that project.

The other dimension of his work is to explore the concept of canon. In his approach, the canon is less a static and fixed entity that is simply given historically than something that is closely tied to the needs of the community for which it functions to provide a sense of identity. He demonstrates the extent to which both the contours of the canon (number, sequence, and arrangement of books) and the textual component of that canon are tied closely to different communities throughout the Second Temple period. Textual variants are closely tied to the needs and the traditions of different communities. More than many scholars, he has always worked hard to make his findings accessible to a broader readership, to complicate their assumptions about the biblical text. This approach is most evident in his books, whereas in his articles and essay-length book reviews, he often seems much freer to address theoretical and methodological issues. In his articles, he pushes the boundaries of how to think about literacy in antiquity, how a scribal curriculum might be elevated to the status of a canonical Scripture, the assumptions that operate in preparing a critical text of the Bible, and the hermeneutical assumptions that govern the technical task of textual criticism. His 2002 coedited volume, *The Canon Debate*, is a valuable resource, with sixteen chapters by leading scholars addressing critical issues involved in the formation of the Old Testament canon and another sixteen addressing the New Testament. The book's title is apt because the articles included take very different approaches and are as polyvalent as the canon that is their subject. Four appendices provide extensive bibliography and list the various canons of the various communities who both share and do not share a common Old Testament and/or New Testament.

VERMES, Geza. "Bible and Midrash: Early Old Testament Exegesis." Pages 199–231 in *The Cambridge History of the Bible*, vol. 1: *From the Beginnings to Jerome.* Edited by Peter R. Ackroyd and C. F. Evans. Cambridge: Cambridge University Press, 1970. Reprinted: pages 59–91 in idem, *Post-Biblical Jewish Studies.* SJLA 8. Leiden: E. J. Brill, 1975.

This brilliant essay turns to the Hebrew Bible to chart the emergence of the kinds of literary and exegetical activity that emerges much more systematically as later rabbinic midrash. VERMES thereby draws upon a model more common in Jewish studies, as a formal category of later rabbinic exegetical commentary upon Scripture, to explain distinctive features of Scripture itself. Indeed, he maintains that this approach helps account for the composition of important works of biblical literature: "It was no doubt a midrashic process . . . which was partly responsible for the formulation of the more recent legal codes, the Deuteronomic and the Priestly, and its influence becomes even more apparent in postexilic literature (Chronicles and Daniel) and certain of the Apocrypha (Ecclesiasticus)" (199). Vermes identifies the kinds of triggers for such midrashic activity, including vocabulary requiring clarification, narrative gaps, and legal ambiguities or inconsistencies.

CHILDS, Brevard S. "Psalm Titles and Midrashic Exegesis." *JSS* 16 (1971): 137–50.

Cooper, Alan M. "The Life and Times of King David according to the Book of Psalms." Pages 117–31 in *The Poet and the Historian: Essays in Literary and Historical Criticism*. Edited by Richard E. Friedman. HSM 26. Chico, Calif.: Scholars Press, 1983.

Slomovic, Elieser. "Toward an Understanding of the Formation of Historical Titles in the Book of the Psalms." *ZAW* 91 (1979): 350–80.

Inner-biblical exegesis has been valuable for explaining the literary connection between the psalm titles (technically termed *superscriptions*) and the psalms. The psalms were normally composed anonymously and then later received a connection with the life of King David, who came to be understood as their author. In this way the psalms, already in the biblical period, were read midrashically and applied to the life of David. At a later period, of course, the church uses a similar process of midrashic rereading to connect the life of David, as narrated by the book of Psalms, to the life of Jesus, interpreted as Davidic scion. For the first stage of this process, see the articles by Childs, Cooper, and Slomovic.

Weinfeld, Moshe. *Deuteronomy and the Deuteronomic School*. Oxford: Clarendon Press, 1972; reprint, Winona Lake, Ind.: Eisenbrauns, 1992.

Weinfeld demonstrates the extent to which the writers of Deuteronomy, posited as professional scribes attached to Josiah's court, drew on a wide range of other biblical literature, both wisdom and law. That approach countered the then dominant form-critical approach to Deuteronomy, which viewed the text's origins in the oral preaching of the rural Levites. With his insight that, technically speaking, Deuteronomy has no (oral) *Sitz im Leben* [setting in life] but rather was the product of scribes working with literary traditions, both biblical and Near Eastern, Weinfeld's work marked a new departure for scholarship on Deuteronomy. True, there are important issues to address (as pointed out by Alexander ROFÉ's review reprinted in idem, *Deuteronomy: Issues and Interpretations* [OTS; Edinburgh: T & T Clark, 2002], 221–30). Nonetheless, he introduced an important new model and, in so doing, provided a crucial foundation for conceptualizing the kind of legal and narrative activity that gave rise to Deuteronomy in terms of inner-biblical exegesis.

WEINGREEN, Jacob. *From Bible to Mishna: The Continuity of Tradition.* Manchester: Manchester University Press, 1976.

Another pioneer in the field of inner-biblical exegesis is WEINGREEN. He demonstrates a clear continuity from biblical material through the formation of the Mishnah, the classical work of Jewish law (ca. 200 C.E.). He demonstrates that Scripture itself arises from this interpretive dimension: that interpretation gives rise to Scripture, and not just vice versa. In particular, he applies this model in a productive way to understand the composition of the book of Deuteronomy. Although some of his work is open to question on matters of dating, the insights that he brings to the text remain valuable.

TALMON, Shemaryahu. "Double Readings in the Massoretic Text." *Textus* 1 (1960): 144–85.

———. "Synonymous Readings in the Textual Tradition of the Old Testament." Pages 335–83 in *Studies in the Bible.* Edited by Chaim Rabin. ScrHier 8. Jerusalem: Magnes, 1961.

———. "The Textual Study of the Bible—A New Outlook." Pages 321–400 in *Qumran and the History of the Biblical Text.*

Edited by Frank Moore Cross and Shemaryahu Talmon. Cambridge, Mass.: Harvard University Press, 1975.
———. "The Presentation of Synchroneity and Simultaneity in Biblical Narrative." Pages 9–26 in *Studies in Hebrew Narrative Art throughout the Ages*. Edited by Joseph Heinemann and Samuel Werses. ScrHier 27. Jerusalem: Magnes, 1978. Reprinted: pages 112–33, in Shemaryahu Talmon, *Literary Studies in the Hebrew Bible: Form and Content*. Jerusalem: Magnes; Leiden: E. J. Brill, 1993.

Shemaryahu Talmon has made major contributions to the understanding of the biblical text and its interpretation, to tracing the development of literary motifs in ancient Israel, and to the use of sociological models to understand sectarianism and the development of the calendar in the Second Temple period. Although he has prepared several volumes of collected essays, some of the rich earlier articles that address the biblical text were not included and deserve mention here. Fittingly, the 1960 article "Double Readings" helped inaugurate *Textus*, the journal affiliated with the important Hebrew University Bible Project, a project initiated by Moshe H. Goshen-Gottstein, and on whose editorial board (along with Chaim Rabin) Talmon has long served. The article demonstrates that the biblical text at a number of points seems to collate two independent readings alongside each other. The scribes responsible for copying and transmitting the biblical text must have become aware of variant traditions or alternative readings from different manuscripts and, instead of choosing between them, retained both.

It is not clear whether this kind of activity was triggered by systematic and self-conscious comparison of different manuscript traditions, with a desire to preserve both, or whether it was more ad hoc, as in the case of a scribe's retaining a memory of an alternative reading. But this model helps explain a number of grammatically or syntactically difficult passages in the biblical text, where scholars might otherwise be inclined to resolve the ostensible redundancy by claiming a literary interpolation or a later editorial layer. As one example, the Covenant Code stipulates the procedure to be used when an Israelite male slave relinquishes the right to manumission: "His master shall take him before God; shall take him before the gate or before the door post" (Exod 21:6). The verse coordinates two clauses, each with identical verb and preposition, both of which specify the locus for the oath to be sworn whereby the slave declines the manumission. It is unnecessary here to claim a later literary layer or interpolation so as to resolve the ostensible redundancy.[6] The "gate" of the Temple or sanctuary was a liminal location where such judicial oaths could be sworn, as is clear from cuneiform law.[7]

Talmon's 1975 article posed an early challenge to the hypothesis associated with Frank Moore Cross that there were three local text families that developed between the fifth and first centuries B.C.E. in Palestine, Egypt, and Babylon. It also questioned whether, for many biblical books, there was ever a single, original "autograph" manuscript, which should be the goal of textual criticism to recover. He argues that there is scant evidence to support such an

[6] Contra Ludger Schwienhorst-Schönberger, *Das Bundesbuch (Ex 20,22–23,33): Studien zu seiner Entstehung und Theologie* (BZAW 188; Berlin: Walter de Gruyter, 1990), 308.

[7] For a fuller discussion, drawing upon Laws of Eshnunna § 37, see Bernard M. Levinson, *Deuteronomy and the Hermeneutics of Legal Innovation* (New York: Oxford University Press, 1997), 114n44.

assumption and proposes a more complex model of different editions of Jeremiah, for example, addressing different communities. Talmon has also done important work exploring the range of functions of scribal devices like the repetitive resumption. The device, also called a *Wiederaufnahme*, was used by ancient scribes to splice a literary insertion or digression into a text. It has a distinctive format: an original sequence A B C, insertion X, then repetition C′, before the original sequence continues as D E F.[8] The structure is the ancient textual equivalent to the technique often employed in modern cinema of using a fade-out to introduce a scene change (as when a character retreats into memory) and then a fade-in to return to the present. Talmon's valuable 1978 article argues that the repetitive resumption was a compositional device used by ancient authors to mark simultaneity of action, not only a sign of secondary editorial layers, as is often maintained. He gathers a number of examples to make this argument, including the account of the revelation of the Ten Commandments at Mount Sinai (Exod 20) to present his case. His parade example, of course, may well point in the opposite direction, given the complex redactional construction of the Sinai pericope. Remarkably, the article shows that medieval rabbinic commentators already recognized the device and described its function. Talmon's contributions enrich the repertoire of the text critic in light of models of exegesis.

[8] On the repetitive resumption and related editorial markers, see Levinson, *Deuteronomy and the Hermeneutics of Legal Innovation*, 17–20.

Blenkinsopp, Joseph. *Prophecy and Canon: A Contribution to the Study of Jewish Origins.* University of Notre Dame Center for the Study of Judaism and Christianity in Antiquity 3. Notre Dame Ind.: University of Notre Dame Press, 1977.

Blenkinsopp, who wrote this volume at a time of an often-apologetic interest in canonical criticism, offers a fresh approach that remains intellectually vigorous. His model of the stages for the emergence and formation of the biblical canon present it as a dynamic process that reflects competition between different communities within Israel and their struggles for power. Those processes are everywhere reflected within the canon, in its divergences of content and in the way its texts respond to one another. Another strength of this model is its critical reflection upon the history of the discipline and constant awareness of the risk of theological bias: "And it is still the case that Christian Old Testament scholars, when they venture beyond a purely descriptive approach to their work, tend to collapse the question of canon into the other question of the relation between the testaments. Nothing has contributed so much as this to the evasion of the ongoing existence of Judaism as a problem for Christian theology" (139).

Eslinger, Lyle. "Hosea 12:5a and Genesis 32:29: A Study in Inner Biblical Exegesis." *JSOT* 18 (1980): 91–99.

Eslinger's study of how the prophet Hosea reuses the Jacob traditions of Genesis, exegetically transforming them, remains stimulating. Especially at the time, it marked a new way of understanding the reuse of this material while applying to it a new model of the prophetic text as a literary interpretation.

FINKELSTEIN, Jacob J. *The Ox That Gored.* Transactions of the American Philosophical Society 71.2. Philadelphia: American Philosophical Society, 1981.

In a brilliant, posthumous monograph, FINKELSTEIN raises the conceptual and methodological stakes. He contends that the conception of human value prevalent in modern Western culture corresponds to and derives from biblical law. In this way, biblical law, despite its chronological antiquity, is already hermeneutically modern. This distinguished Assyriologist argues that ostensibly minute differences of sequence or legal sanction between biblical and Near Eastern law reflect the drafter's attempt to distinguish between person and property. In a richly suggestive analysis, he argues that the drafter's focus on the category of person is apparent in the organization of the Covenant Code and even helps explain shifts of topic that have otherwise been viewed as intrusive or secondary. The author of the Covenant Code in this way rereads the judicial norms and literary conventions of cuneiform law. Biblical law thus represents something like a philosophical argument. It conceptualizes the autonomy and the sovereignty of the person. Finkelstein follows the history of related ideas into the legal systems of antiquity, medieval Europe, and contemporary American law.

LEMAIRE, André. *Les écoles et la formation de la Bible dans l'ancien Israël.* OBO 39. Fribourg, Switzerland: Éditions Universitaires; Göttingen: Vandenhoeck & Ruprecht, 1981.

At a time when many scholars in the discipline remained enamored by the model of the Bible as an oral literature, André LEMAIRE should be saluted for having raised the entire question of literacy in ancient Israel. Drawing upon his expertise in the study of Semitic inscriptions, he sought to integrate epigraphy with the analysis of the biblical text. He argued that many inscriptions represent instructional texts used for training in the scribal schools, the existence of which he posited during the Israelite monarchy. According to this model, the Hebrew Bible originally represents a series of texts that were copied, transmitted, and studied in these schools. The texts were eventually collated and gained the status of a literary canon. Although aspects of this proposal require revision based upon subsequent scholarship, his ability to break away from the assumption of an exclusively oral *Sitz im Leben* to account for Israelite literature makes a lasting contribution to the field. Unfortunately, this study has sometimes been overlooked by other scholars working on literacy in ancient Israel (see SCHNIEDEWIND 2004).

FISHBANE, Michael. "Torah and Tradition." Pages 275–300 in *Tradition and Theology in the Old Testament*. Edited by Douglas A. Knight. Philadelphia: Fortress, 1977.

———. *Biblical Interpretation in Ancient Israel*. Oxford: Clarendon Press, 1985; with addenda, 1988.

———. "Use, Authority, and Interpretation of Mikra at Qumran." Pages 339–77 in *Mikra: Text, Translation, Reading, and Interpretation of the Hebrew Bible in Ancient Judaism and Early Christianity*. Edited by Martin J. Mulder. CRINT 2.1. Assen/Maastricht: Van Gorcum; Philadelphia: Fortress, 1988.

———. "The Hebrew Bible and Exegetical Tradition." Pages 15–30 in *Intertextuality in Ugarit and Israel*. Edited by Johannes C. de Moor. Oudtestamentische Studiën 40. Leiden: E. J. Brill, 1998.

———. *Biblical Myth and Rabbinic Mythmaking*. Oxford: Oxford University Press, 2003.

FISHBANE, building on the insights of a number of other scholars, provides a new model for analyzing the composition and growth of biblical literature. He demonstrates the extent to which Israelite scribes and authors were constrained to comment upon, explicate, annotate, revise, refer to, and embellish earlier texts that occupied a privileged place in their culture. In doing so, Fishbane shows how the dynamic of tradition and interpretation is not only a postbiblical but also an inner-biblical one. The continuities of literary form and exegetical technique, which reach from cuneiform literature through biblical texts into the Dead Sea Scrolls, imply that the exegetical techniques of rabbinic literature presuppose an immanent tradition of textual study and do not belatedly derive from the Greco-Roman culture of late antiquity. The book also establishes continuities of form and scribal technique that span the various literary genres of the Bible. His analysis of the reinterpretation of the Hebrew Bible in the Dead Sea Scrolls in the *Mikra* [the Hebrew term for *Bible*, derived from "what is read"] volume provides a comprehensive and engaging introduction. He contextualizes the nature of the legal, prophetic, and narrative reworking attested at Qumran in light of the exegetical techniques that were employed in cuneiform literature and in the Bible. He demonstrates clear continuities of both form and technique, connecting the *pesher* material, for example, with the terminology for and the techniques of dream and omen interpretation attested in Akkadian literature and, within the Bible, in the Joseph stories and Daniel. He pays careful attention to the nature of lemmatic interpretation (including atomistic citation and use of deictic pronouns) and to means for authorizing exegetical transformations (including pseudepigraphy).

In the 1998 edited volume, Fishbane reflects upon his major work of 1985, now with more than a decade of hindsight. He seeks to push beyond his earlier methodological distinction between *traditum*, or the received tradition, and *traditio*, the dynamic process of its transmission and transformation:

> [T]he Bible is only tradition, in form and content. . . . As we now have them, we have tradition producing tradition through the mediation of a silent redaction. This silent hand of culture-formation and its anthological product is of the essence of biblical and post-biblical tradition. (18)

The larger goal of this scholarly analysis is a project of cultural recovery: "the Hebrew Bible is the product of tradition in diverse stages of unfolding, and . . . to catch the content in diverse contexts would be to penetrate beneath the textual surface to the living reality of Israel" (ibid.).

Fishbane's concern with the subsurface culture that underlies the biblical text serves as the point of departure for his next major work, *Biblical Myth and Mythmaking*. The volume is a significant contribution to the history of religion. Scholars as well as laity tend to make a sharp distinction between mythological religions and monotheism, as if the former were more primitive and irrational and the monotheistic religions had to replace and move beyond them to achieve their distinctive identity. This basic model also applied to the emergence of academic Jewish studies in Germany during the nineteenth century, where *Wissenschaft des Judentums*, seeking the full assimilation and integration of Jews into German society, presented Judaism as a religion of complete rationality, almost as if it were the original Kantian religion.[9] Fishbane makes a

[9] The claim that accommodation and assimilation were the goals of *Wissenschaft des Judentums* is associated primarily with the position of Gershom Scholem. For a comprehensive assessment, see Jonathan

strong argument that myth is integral to both monotheism and Judaism. The volume is a demanding, often-technical read that covers two millennia of literary history. Its three major sections focus upon ancient Israel, the midrashic literature of rabbinic Judaism, and medieval Judaism (with particular attention to the Zohar in the twelfth and thirteenth centuries, in Provence, Gerona, and Castile). In each case, Fishbane investigates two different modes of conceptualizing God: the cosmological acts of God (God as creator) and the *magnalia dei*, the great acts of God in history as he defends or redeems Israel (Yahweh as Divine Warrior). Through all of this, he seeks to realign some of the standard intellectual categories. Myth becomes a form of exegesis, and Jewish history becomes a series of ever intensifying rereadings of the past. Ancient Israelite authors rework Near Eastern material to conceptualize creation or redemption; rabbinic authorities reread the biblical canon to turn it into a kind of lexicon for new mythmaking (to depict the Shekinah as going into slavery in Egypt along with Israel, so that God is then redeemed along with his people in the Exodus); and in the Zoharic rereading, the canon of Scripture itself finally becomes only a coded textual metaphor for God, depicted as embodied, as having an erotic life, and as being affected directly by human action and historical events such as the destruction of the Temple. In this ambitious study, exegesis is no longer a specific textual interpretation. It becomes a form of

Frankel, "Assimilation and the Jews in Nineteenth-Century Europe: Towards a New Historiography," in *Assimilation and Community: The Jews in Nineteenth Century Europe* (ed. Jonathan Frankel and Steven J. Zipperstein; Cambridge: Cambridge University Press, 1992), 1–37.

cultural transformation and religious imagination central to monotheism.

Levin, Christoph. *Die Verheißung des neuen Bundes: in ihrem theologiegeschichtlichen Zusammenhang ausgelegt.* FRLANT 137. Göttingen: Vandenhoeck & Ruprecht, 1985.

In contemporary scholarship, Christoph Levin has come primarily to be associated with the ferment in pentateuchal theory. He was an early advocate for the tendency to redate the Yahwist to the exilic period, subsequent to Deuteronomy but prior to the Deuteronomistic History.[10] Similarly, he regards the Yahwist not as the author of an ancient primary source but as a late editor who worked with received literary materials to give them shape. These more recent debates should not obscure his striking contribution to the interpretation of the prophetic corpus, which takes issue with the then-dominant models for analyzing the composition and structure of Jeremiah by stressing the importance of inner-biblical exegesis:

Jeder einzelne Abschnitt der Prophetenbücher zerfällt bei kritischem Zugriff in zahlreiche literarische Schichten, und es ist vergebliche Mühe, jede dieser Schichten einer Redaktion zuzuordnen, die die systematische Bearbeitung eines ganzen Buches umfaßt. Es muß deutlich sein: Sobald

[10] See Christoph Levin, *Der Jahwist* (FRLANT 157; Göttingen: Vandenhoeck & Ruprecht, 1993); and, most recently, idem, "The Yahwist: The Earliest Editor of the Pentateuch," *JBL* 126 (2007): 209–30. On the matter of the literary sequence and the dating, I reach different conclusions based upon an analysis of the altar law of the Covenant Code (Exod 20:24); see Bernard M. Levinson, "Is the Covenant Code an Exilic Composition? A Response to John Van Seters," in idem, *"The Right Chorale": Studies in Biblical Law and Interpretation* (FAT 54; Tübingen: Mohr Siebeck, 2008), 276–330.

eine Erstredaktion ihr Werk getan hat oder eine beliebige Sammlung von Prophetenworten vorliegt, ist die Matrize für beliebige literarische Zusätze vorhanden. . . . Pointiert kann man sagen: Die prophetische Literatur, ja mit Einschränkung das ganze Alte Testament, ist in erster Linie weder Autoren- noch Redaktorenliteratur, sondern Auslegungsliteratur, ein großer, in Jahrhunderten gewachsener, schriftlicher Midrasch: "Sacra scriptura sui ipsius interpres."[11]

[Each individual unit of the prophetic corpus gets broken down by means of critical incursion into numerous literary strata, and it is so much wasted effort to assign each of these strata to a particular redaction that spans the editing of the entire book. It becomes clear: no sooner than a first redaction has been prepared or a random collection of prophetic words is at hand, it then provides the matrix for random literary additions. . . . One can say, more pointedly: *The prophetic corpus—indeed, the entire Old Testament—should be understood in the first instance as the work neither of authors nor of redactors but as exegetical literature: as a major, written Midrash that grew up over several centuries.* "Sacred Scripture is its own interpreter"].

Levin's elegant suture of Jewish terminology with Luther's famous motto is itself, of course, a form of midrashic rereading. As he seeks to reorient conventional approaches to the formation of Jeremiah, he assigns his approach a strong and ecumenical pedigree while seeking to trump the more established history of scholarship. Indeed, approaches remarkably similar to his began to

[11] Levin, *Verheißung des neuen Bundes*, 67 (my translation follows, emphasis added). Also cited by Schmid, "Innerbiblische Schriftauslegung: Aspekte der Forschungsgeschichte," 17 (see entry herein).

be applied more broadly around this time, even if not directly dependent upon Levin's proposal. William McKane argued that the formation of Jeremiah is best described as a "rolling corpus." "What is meant by a rolling *corpus* is that small pieces of pre-existing text trigger exegesis or commentary. MT is to be understood as a commentary or commentaries built on pre-existing elements of the Jeremianic *corpus*."[12] In the discussion earlier of the reworking of Deuteronomy 24 by Ezekiel 18, I found myself coming to different conclusions about the direction of literary development than Levin had earlier proposed, but there was a shared understanding that it is indeed an exegetical process that is at issue.

TIGAY, Jeffrey H., ed. *Empirical Models for Biblical Criticism.* Philadelphia: University of Pennsylvania, 1985.

TIGAY's edited volume is exciting to work through. It spans literature from the ancient Near East (Gilgamesh, the Laws of Hammurabi), the Hebrew Bible, and postbiblical literature (the Samaritan Pentateuch and the Septuagint). The explicit goal is to show the immanent nature of the source-critical model (as completely anchored in the literary and scribal conventions of the time). This is done very effectively. Although the whole volume contains valuable contributions from several other scholars, the focus here is on Tigay's own three chapters: "The Evolution of

[12] William McKane, *A Critical and Exegetical Commentary on Jeremiah* (2 vols.; ICC; Edinburgh: T. & T. Clark, 1986–1996), 1:lxxxiii (emphasis in original). Levin's work, published a year earlier, is not cited there or elsewhere in vol. 1; there are frequent references to it, however, in vol. 2. The similarity is also cited by SCHMID, "Innerbiblische Schriftauslegung: Aspekte der Forschungsgeschichte," 17.

the Pentateuchal Narratives in the Light of the Evolution of the *Gilgamesh Epic*" (21–52), "Conflation as a Redactional Technique" (53–96), and "The Stylistic Criterion of Source Criticism in the Light of Ancient Near Eastern and Postbiblical Literature" (150–73). The first traces the long development of the Gilgamesh Epic and shows the important role of an ancient scholar, Sîn-lēqqi-unninni, in giving the work its distinctive form and content.[13] In the second chapter specified, Tigay provides a fascinating analysis of how the authors of the Samaritan Pentateuch, working sometime in the first or second century B.C.E., composed a "counter-Pentateuch," seeking to legitimate their community and their sanctuary at Shechem (Mount Gerizim, located near modern Nablus).[14] The remarkable thing is that they did so simply by making strategic alterations to an earlier form of the Jewish Torah. Hardly any new explicitly sectarian material needed to be composed from whole cloth. Instead, the skilled editors of the work essentially only "copied and pasted" already-existing material recognizing the importance of Shechem (see Deut 11 and 27) into the Tenth Commandment of the Decalogue. They thereby wrote their revision of the Torah into the Torah,

[13] Tigay here provides a précis of his earlier monograph, *The Evolution of the Gilgamesh Epic* (Philadelphia: University of Pennsylvania Press, 1982). Since that publication, more tablets have been discovered. For the most recent treatment (and with a discussion of the role of Sîn-lēqqi-unninni), see now Andrew R. George, *The Babylonian Gilgamesh Epic: Introduction, Critical Edition, and Cuneiform Texts* (2 vols.; Oxford: Oxford University Press, 2003), 1:28–33.

[14] For the most recent study, addressing both textual and historical issues, see Reinhard Pummer, "The Samaritans and Their Pentateuch," in *The Pentateuch as Torah: New Models for Understanding Its Promulgation and Acceptance* (ed. Gary N. Knoppers and Bernard M. Levinson; Winona Lake, Ind.: Eisenbrauns, 2007), 237–69.

making their rejection of Jerusalem and affirmation of Gerizim derive from Sinaitic revelation. Tigay does a superb job of showing the meticulous scribal techniques involved in this major ideological statement. This approach has broader significance, given that the Pentateuch itself in its final form is a Second Temple redactional composition. It is possible to demonstrate similar techniques involved in the composition of key passages within the Pentateuch itself (see ZAHN entry herein). The third chapter specified demonstrates how the source-critical model, far from being an anachronistic, rationalistic, and Western imposition onto the biblical text is consistent with the techniques employed in the composition of both Near Eastern and Second Temple literature more broadly.

KUGEL, James L. "Early Interpretation: The Common Background of Late Forms of Biblical Exegesis." Pages 9–106 in *Early Biblical Interpretation.* Edited by James L. Kugel and Rowan Greer. Philadelphia: Westminster, 1986.

———. *Traditions of the Bible: A Guide to the Bible As It Was at the Start of the Common Era.* Cambridge: Harvard University Press, 1998.

A gifted writer, KUGEL is very much alive to how Scripture gives rise to interpretation, which then becomes itself a new form of religious activity. The extent to which the formative literature of the multiple "Judaisms" of the Second Temple period, including the Dead Sea Scrolls, rabbinic Judaism, and Christianity, respond to issues in the biblical text is something that he illuminates. His focus is almost completely on the reception of biblical material by later interpretive communities; the significance of this approach for the compositional history of the biblical material is more directly addressed in the work of other scholars. The earlier volume provides a clear introduction to the important categories of the emergence of textual interpretation as a replacement for prophecy in the Second Temple period within ancient Israel, with the result that the inspired interpreter in a way replaces the prophet as the divine spokesperson to the community. The later volume positions the Hebrew Bible in the context of the various communities of religious readers and interpreters in the Second Temple period. The focus here is indeed to provide access to the Bible "as it was at the start of the Common Era." The volume "keys" the study of a wide range of Second Temple literature to the biblical texts that it responds to and seeks to illuminate. Both books are written for a broad audience and are very accessible.

LOHFINK, Norbert. "Die Sicherung der Wirksamkeit des Gotteswortes durch das Prinzip der Schriftlichkeit der Tora und durch das Prinzip der Gewaltenteilung nach den Ämtergesetzen des Buches Deuteronomium (Dt 16,18–18,22)." Pages 143–55 in *Testimonium Veritati: Festschrift Wilhelm Kempf*. Edited by H. Wolter. Frankfurter Theologische Studien 7. Frankfurt: Knecht, 1971. Reprinted: pages 305–23 in idem, *Studien zum Deuteronomium und zur deuteronomistischen Literatur I*. SBAB 8. Stuttgart: Katholisches Bibelwerk, 1990. Translated as "Distribution of the Functions of Power: The Laws Concerning Public Offices in Deuteronomy 16:18–18:22." Pages 336–52 in *A Song of Power and the Power of Song: Essays on the Book of Deuteronomy*. Edited by Duane L. Christensen, Winona Lake, Ind.: Eisenbrauns, 1993.

———. "Gab es eine deuteronomistische Bewegung?" Pages 313–82 in *Jeremia und die "deuteronomistische Bewegung."* Edited by Walter Groβ. BBB 98. Weinheim: Beltz Athenaum, 1995. Reprinted: pages 65–142 in idem, *Studien zum Deuteronomium und zur deuteronomistischen Literatur III*. SBAB 20. Stuttgart: Katholisches Bibelwerk, 1995. Abridged translation: "Was There a Deuteronomistic Movement?"

Pages 36–66 in *Those Elusive Deuteronomists: The Phenomenon of Pan-Deuteronomism*. Edited by Linda S. Shearing and Steven L. McKenzie. JSOTSup 268. Sheffield: Sheffield Academic Press, 1999.

———. "Fortschreibung? Zur Technik vom Rechtsrevisionen im deuteronomischen Bereich, erörtert an Deuteronomium 12, Ex 21,2–11 und Dtn 15,12–18." Pages 133–81 in *Das Deuteronomium und seine Querbeziehungen*. Edited by Timo Veijola. Schriften der Finnischen Exegetischen Gesellschaft 62. Göttingen: Vandenhoeck & Ruprecht, 1996. Reprinted: pages 163–203 in idem, *Studien zum Deuteronomium und zur deuteronomistischen Literatur IV.* SBAB 31. Stuttgart: Katholisches Bibelwerk, 2000.

———. "Prolegomena zu einer Rechtshermeneutik des Pentateuch." Pages 11–55 in *Das Deuteronomium*. Edited by Georg Braulik. ÖBS 23. Frankfurt: Peter Lang, 2003. Reprinted: pages 181–231 in Norbert Lohfink, *Studien zum Deuteronomium und zur deuteronomistischen Literatur* V. SBAB 38; Stuttgart: Katholisches Bibelwerk, 2005.

Having devoted his life to the study of Deuteronomy, LOHFINK has in many ways revolutionized the study of that important biblical book. He was one of the very first to recognize and stress its literary artistry and rhetorical structure. In doing so, he sought to create an implicit dialogue between standard continental diachronic approaches (source-critical and text-critical) and the methodology of contemporary literary studies. One of his early studies, the German original of which was written in the excitement associated with Vatican II, argues that certain key concepts associated with democratic government (the separation of powers and the subordination of all governmental bodies to the constitution or the rule of law) originates with Deuteronomy. That article provides a fascinating extended meditation upon the concept of Torah in Deuteronomy. The "Fortschreibung?"

article provides a close reading of several key legal texts in the Covenant Code and Deuteronomy, thinking through with wonderful clarity how to understand their literary relationship. Stress is placed on the rules for the sacrificial worship of God (the altar laws of Exod 20:24 and Deut 12) and the manumission laws (Exod 21:2–11; Deut 15:12–18). The article demonstrates the exegetical power of the author of Deuteronomy, as he fundamentally transforms the literary model of the Covenant Code: placing new wine in old skins. Another aspect of the article is equally important. Quite self-consciously, it reflects upon the different theoretical models used to account for inner-biblical interpretation. Using the specified texts as a series of test cases, Lohfink argues that the conventional continental model of *Fortschreibung* (as employed particularly by Eckart Otto) envisions straightforward extensions to or adjustments of a source text while nonetheless preserving it intact. This model fails to do justice to the much more dynamic reworking of the Covenant Code by Deuteronomy. Lohfink implicitly calls for the more powerful model of exegesis. His reading powerfully demonstrates that legal rewriting and revision is an act of originality and authorship in the strong sense. In the important article published in 1995, Lohfink mounts a powerful and sustained challenge to the standard scholarly model, one especially prevalent in European contexts, that isolates discrete strata of Deuteronomistic redactional activity in the prophetic corpus, on the basis of minor variations of language, and then reconstructs (without other evidence) a distinct social and religious movement. Rather than assume that each variation of language represents the fingerprints of a specific social group, or stages of that group's development,

Lohfink assumes a much greater capacity for authors, in working with texts, to vary their language. He argues that such ancient authors would almost certainly imitate the language of the literary sources upon which they draw. From this perspective, any stylistic variation (including grammatical inconsistencies) found in their sources could well become a kind of literary model to be used in the creation of new literature. In the 2003 article, Lohfink's point of departure is the hermeneutical problem created by the remarkable redacted nature of the Pentateuch itself, which includes three originally inconsistent, independent, and mutually exclusive legal collections (the Covenant Code, the Holiness Code, and the legal corpus of Deuteronomy) while granting each equal authority. Lohfink astutely asks, How could such a text have been read in antiquity? He explores how a hypothetical first reader might have understood the Pentateuch from the moment after its creation. Lohfink and Georg Braulik (note the discussion of his work in the section on Ruth) are preparing the new Hermeneia commentary on Deuteronomy, with the first volume devoted to Deuteronomy 1–4. With attention to both synchronic and diachronic issues, to how the book would have been read in the context of the canon, and to how it rereads earlier biblical literature, the volume promises to be an indispensable contribution to the field.

Steck, Odil Hannes. *Bereitete Heimkehr: Jesaja 35 als Redaktionelle Brücke zwischen dem Ersten und dem Zweiten Jesaja.* SBS 121. Stuttgart: Katholisches Bibelwerk, 1985.

———. *Der Abschluss der Prophetie im Alten Testament: Ein Versuch zur Frage der Vorgeschichte des Kanons.* BThSt 17. Neukirchen-Vluyn: Neukirchener Verlag, 1991.

———. *The Prophetic Books and their Theological Witness.* Translated by James D. Nogalski. St. Louis: Chalice, 2000.

———. *Gott in der Zeit entdecken: Die Prophetenbücher des Alten Testaments als Vorbild für Theologie und Kirche.* BThSt 42. Neukirchen-Vluyn: Neukirchener Verlag, 2001.

An important development within scholarship on inner-biblical exegesis is represented by the work of Odil Hannes STECK. Unfortunately, only one of Steck's volumes has been translated into English, and the major work is available only in German. As a result, the primary contributions of his approach tend to be known only to specialists working on the formation of the book of Isaiah (Deutero- and Trito-Isaiah) and the formation of the Book of the Twelve (the so-called minor prophets). A broader dialogue with scholarship on inner-biblical exegesis to compare methodological assumptions has not yet taken place. I hope that the remarks here can contribute to such a comparison of intellectual models. Several scholars who have trained with Steck have gone on to build on and develop his insights in independent ways, extending them in new directions. These include Reinhard G. KRATZ, James D. Nogalski,[15] Erich Bosshard-Nepustil, and Konrad SCHMID. Although there have been inevitable suggestions that Steck and his followers constitute a Zürich school, the range of approaches and historical interests is too diverse to sustain such a generalization.[16]

The perception of a school derives from a distinctive model for understanding the formation of the prophetic

[15] See James D. Nogalski, *Literary Precursors to the Book of the Twelve* (BZAW 217; Berlin: Walter de Gruyter, 1993); and James D. Nogalski and Marvin A. Sweeney, eds., *Reading and Hearing the Book of the Twelve* (SBLSymS 15; Atlanta: Society of Biblical Literature, 2000).

[16] Contra Rainer Kessler, review of Odil Hannes Steck, *Die Prophetenbücher und ihr theologischer Zeugnis: Wege der Nachfrage und Fährten zur Antwort, TLZ* 123 (1998): 370–71.

corpus as the result of an extended process of inner-biblical *Rezeptionsgeschichte* [reception history]. This approach understands the formation of individual prophetic books, and even of larger literary units (such as the Book of the Twelve) to represent studied responses to earlier prophecy that then become systematized and given shape as a cohesive redaction of the book. An example of the former approach is Schmid's *Buchgestalten des Jeremiabuches* (1996), which presents the formation of the book of Jeremiah as a series of successive editions, each of which sought to interpret, reapply, and contemporize the earlier Jeremianic material. An example of the latter approach is Steck's *Der Abschluß der Prophetie im Alten Testament: Ein Versuch zur Frage der Vorgeschichte des Kanons* [The Closure of Prophecy in the Old Testament: An Attempt at the Question of the Prehistory of the Canon] or Bosshard-Nepustil's *Rezeptionen von Jesaja 1–39 im Zwölfprophetenbuch* [The Reception of Isaiah 1–39 in the Book of the Twelve].[17] Steck and Bosshard-Nepustil maintain that the book of Isaiah and the Book of the Twelve were aligned with one another, substantively and theologically, in the process of their transmission. These scholars argue that, as each of these compositions took shape as books, they influenced the formation of the other in language, structure, and ideas.

With this macro model of redaction, Steck argued against dominant continental European approaches to *Redaktionsgeschichte* [redaction history], which he rejected

[17] For an in-depth analysis, see Marvin A. Sweeney, review of Erich Bosshard-Nepustil, *Rezeptionen von Jesaja 1–39 im Zwölfprophetenbuch: Untersuchungen zur literarischen Verbindung von Prophetenbüchern in babylonischer und persischer Zeit*, *RBL* (1999), http://www.bookreviews.org; cited September 22, 2007.

for being historically naive in its obsession to gain "swift access to the prophet" (*Prophetic Books*, xi) while ignoring the extent to which the prophet is also a construction of the book. He also was dismissive of the atomistic microanalyses of this approach, which often failed to examine the significance of the final form of the book as an important theological statement and source of historical evidence.

Steck equally sought to distinguish his approach to the *Redaktion* of the prophetical books from *Fortschreibung* [updating; lit., "writing forth" or "extrapolating"], another well-known concept, especially in continental biblical scholarship. The latter would refer to small-scale inner-biblical expansions or extrapolations that elucidate an individual sentence or literary unit with a later explanatory comment, such as the originally unidentified "all the peoples of the kingdoms of the north" who are to visit destruction upon Judah (Jer 1:5) being specified, in light of historical hindsight, as "all the peoples of the north . . . *and my servant, King Nebuchadrezzar of Babylon*" (Jer 25:9). In contrast, he always connects redaction to a form of exegesis that affects the structure of an entire book. For example, he regards Isaiah 35 as a linchpin that was, from the very beginning, composed to join first Isaiah (Isa 1–39) and Deutero-Isaiah together into a single, larger composition. This builds on the insights of a previous generation of scholars, who were able to identify Isaiah 35 as an interpolation into first Isaiah of material linguistically and theologically associated with Deutero-Isaiah.[18] Rather than view the chapter as a textual disruption, Steck argues that

[18] See Heinrich Graetz, "Isaiah XXXIV and XXXV," *JQR* 4 (1891): 1–8; and Charles C. Torrey, *The Second Isaiah: A New Interpretation* (New York: Charles Scribner's Sons, 1928), 53.

the chapter plays a constitutive role in the formation of the book of Isaiah, understood now as a conscious literary and theological creation, one that is a product of inner-biblical exegesis. According to this model, inner-biblical exegesis becomes not only a form of reading and interpretation within the Bible but also a process that gives rise to and helps explain a biblical book's distinctive structure.[19]

The different approaches emerge perhaps most clearly in regard to the treatment of the book of Isaiah. Steck and his successors not only have investigated selective and specific textual units as examples of inner-biblical exegesis (for example, the way that Isa 56 reworks and reinterprets the restrictive rules for admission into the community found in Deut 23[20]) but also see much larger textual units as providing the points of departure for inner-biblical exegesis. Steck and his successors attempt, in addition, to find

[19] Steck's distinction seems to overlook the kind of work that has been done on biblical law and the Pentateuch. Several decades ago, WEINGREEN, and more recently, OTTO and I have argued that exegetical activity gives rise to the content and the structure of larger textual units like the legal corpus of Deuteronomy and the Holiness Code.

[20] For the original publication of this idea in the German-speaking world, see Herbert Donner, "Jesaja LVI 1–7: Ein Abrogationsfall innerhalb des Kanons—Implikationen und Konsequenzen," in *Congress Volume, Salamanca 1983* (ed. J. A. Emerton; VTSup 36; Leiden: E. J. Brill, 1985), 81–95; reprint, idem, *Aufsätze zum Alten Testament aus vier Jahrzehnten* (BZAW 224; Berlin: Walter de Gruyter, 1994), 165–79. Ironically, a similar analysis was published the same year by Michael Fishbane, addressing the conflicting rules for inclusion/exclusion of the foreigner from the community in Ezek 44:6–9, Isa 56:1–8, Num 18, and, more briefly, Deut 23 (*Biblical Interpretation in Ancient Israel* [Oxford: Clarendon, 1985], 118–19; 138–43 [esp. 142n98). See Joachim SCHAPER's entry herein for a careful study addressing methodological issues that integrates these various approaches.

theological and conceptional *Leitfossilien* [index fossils] to provide what they consider reliable historical reference points as guides in reconstructing the literary history of a book: how is Israel regarded, and how is the relationship of Israel to other nations understood, etc. There is, of course, an obvious risk of circularity, inasmuch as prior conceptions about ideas of ethnic particularity and universalism, and whether one way of thinking develops into another or whether divergent ideas held by different groups circulated in the population at the same time, can easily control the historical construction.

Benjamin SOMMER's recent *A Prophet Reads Scripture* (see the entry herein) helps provide a useful contrast, given his rich analysis of the range of exegetical strategies that are employed in Isaiah. Sommer's observation that the exegetical techniques evident in Isaiah 40–66 are largely consistent leads him to the conclusion that this entire corpus derives from a single author. In other words, on the basis of an analysis of exegetical form, he does not accept the distinction between Deutero-Isaiah (Isa 40–55) and Trito-Isaiah (Isa 56–66). The approach of Steck, Kratz, and Schmid, in contrast, pays more attention to the content and statement of the exegesis. Here the goal is to identify the discontinuities evident in the conception of the nation and its relationship to other nations and thereby to reaffirm the more conventional literary demarcation, while at the same time exploring how this material became integrated into a single, larger book.

Steck had a strong commitment to the implications of his research for contemporary work in theology. The affirmation of the vitality of tradition became a corrective to strong commitment to *sola scriptura*. Rather than theological truth being restricted to the fossilized words of an ancient text, he believed that the process of interpretation and actualization that gave shape to the prophetic corpus in antiquity provides a warrant to the ongoing hermeneutical task of making Scripture relevant to the present day. The application of his model for the inner-biblical reception and reinterpretation of earlier texts to current theological issues is the focus of the second half of *The Prophetic Books and their Theological Witness*. The same topic receives monograph length attention in *Gott in der Zeit entdecken*, published in the year of his death to cancer at age sixty-six.

Kratz, Reinhard Gregor. *Kyros im Deuterojesaja-Buch: Redaktionsgeschichtliche Untersuchungen zu Entstehung und Theologie von Jes 40–55*. FAT 1. Tübingen: Mohr-Siebeck, 1991.

———. "Redaktionsgeschichte/Redaktionskritik I." Pages 367–78 in vol. 28 (1997) of *Theologische Realenzyklopädie*. Edited by Gerhard Krause and Gerhard Müller. 36 vols. Berlin and New York: Walter de Gruyter, 1977–2004.

———. "Die Entstehung des Judentums: Zur Kontroverse zwischen E. Meyer und J. Wellhausen." Pages 1–22 in idem, *Das Judentum im Zeitalter des Zweiten Tempels*. FAT 42. Tübingen: Mohr Siebeck, 2004.

———. "Innerbiblische Exegese und Redaktionsgeschicte im Lichte empirischer Evidenz." Pages 126–56 in idem, *Das Judentum im Zeitalter des Zweiten Tempels*. FAT 42. Tübingen: Mohr Siebeck, 2004.

———. "Temple and Torah: Reflections on the Legal Status of the Pentateuch between Elephantine and Qumran." Pages 77–104 in *The Pentateuch as Torah: New Models for Understanding Its Promulgation and Acceptance*. Edited by Gary N. Knoppers and Bernard M. Levinson. Winona Lake, Ind.: Eisenbrauns, 2007.

Wie die Ausbildung des vorexilischen Jahvismus, das Auftreten, die Ideen und die Wirkung der Propheten nur verständlich sind auf dem Hintergrund der grossen Weltbegebenheiten, die sich in Vorderasien abspielen, so ist die Entstehung des Judenthums nur zu begreifen als Produkt des Perserreichs.[21]

[Just as the formation of preexilic Yahwism (and) the appearance, ideas, and impact of the prophets are only intelligible against the background of the major events that took place in the Near East, so is the emergence of Judaism conceivable only as the product of the Persian Empire.]

The preceding citation is drawn from the historian Eduard Meyer's *Die Entstehung des Judenthums.* In 1897, the year after Meyer published his volume, Julius Wellhausen retorted that he had published essentially the same idea in 1884 and that Meyer was saying nothing new. He acerbically dismissed the relevance of the allegedly decisive external evidence of the Persian Empire: "Das wissen wir aus dem Alten Testament; die übrigen Quellen machen uns nicht klüger" [We know that from the Old Testament; the remaining sources do not make us more knowledgeable].[22] The exchange between the two provides the point of departure for Reinhard KRATZ's essay, "Die Entstehung des Judentums," his *Antrittsvorlesung* [inaugural lecture] as *Ordinarius* at George August University in Göttingen,

[21] Eduard Meyer, *Die Entstehung des Judenthums: Eine historische Untersuchung* (Halle: Max Niemeyer, 1896), 71; 2d reprint as *Die Entstehung des Judenthums: Eine historische Untersuchung; Julius Wellhausen und meine Schrift, "Die Entstehung des Judentums": Eine Erwiderung* (Hildesheim: Georg Olms, 1987), 71. Cited by Kratz, "Entstehung des Judentums," 6 (my translation follows).

[22] Julius Wellhausen, review of Eduard Meyer, *Die Entstehung des Judenthums*, in *Göttingischen gelehrten Anzeigen* 159 (1897): 89–97 (at 96). Cited by Kratz, "Entstehung des Judentums," 7 (my translation).

where Wellhausen taught when he wrote his response to Meyer.

The essay opens a window into the history of ideas that is insufficiently known. It bears directly upon the focus of the current book because it immediately raises the question of the relationship between history and hermeneutics: To what extent do the kind of textual phenomena that are investigated by means of inner-biblical exegesis contribute to the understanding of the history of ancient Israel and the broader Second Temple period? Does a sound historiography base itself exclusively upon external and objective events and documentary sources, to the exclusion of the literary material of the Hebrew Bible for which there is such a striking absence of external sources? Do the documents of exegesis have significance for historiography? How are the two to be integrated? These methodological questions, which continue to occupy the field, were already a point of active debate at the end of the nineteenth century.

Mediating between the external and the internal, between the world of history and the insights of hermeneutics, represents the continuing theme of Kratz's scholarship. The concise article "Redaktionsgeschichte/Redaktionskritik" shows the extent to which different conceptions of redaction provide one way to trace the history of biblical scholarship, from the classical methods of the nineteenth-century literary critics (who thought in terms of documents) through the approach of tradition-historical scholarship (the structuring and arrangement of originally oral short units), to the newer approaches associated with Odil Hannes Steck. Here redaction is shown also to be a form of interpretation, but one that also responds to external historical events and in turn points to them. Kratz's 1991 Zürich Habilitation (second dissertation) takes a similar approach, arguing that two different conceptions of Cyrus in Deutero-Isaiah (Cyrus as God's anointed, appointed to overthrow Babylon; and Cyrus as God's servant, appointed to serve as a light to the nations) represent two distinct literary layers that have been brought together. Although the question could be raised of whether the two concepts need be mutually exclusive, Kratz's detailed reading seeks to show how the redactional structure of Isaiah 40–55 points to and sheds light on the historical context for the book's composition. His study of inner-biblical exegesis, discussed earlier, covers *pesher* literature, quotation and rewritten Bible, text and versions, and redaction while seeking to provide external analogics for the phenomena he describes. The 2007 article argues that the phenomena of hermeneutics—the biblical text, as artifact and as object of community self-definition—themselves give rise to further historical developments, including sectarianism. Kratz situates the promulgation of the Torah, chronologically as well as conceptually, between Elephantine (where there was a temple but no Torah) and Qumran (where there was a Torah but no temple). Between those two extremes, he maintains, the Torah may be found.

Zakovitch, Yair. *An Introduction to Inner-Biblical Interpretation.* Even Yehudah: Rekhes, 1992 (Hebrew).

———. "The Book of the Covenant explains the Book of the Covenant: The 'Boomerang Phenomenon.'" Pages 59–64 in *Texts, Temples and Traditions.* Edited by Michael V. Fox et al. Winona Lake, Ind.: Eisenbrauns, 1996 (Hebrew).

———. "Poetry Creates Historiography." Pages 311–20 in *"A Wise and Discerning Mind": Essays in Honor of Burke O. Long.* Edited by Saul M. Olyan and Robert C. Culley. BJS 325. Providence, R.I.: Brown Judaic Studies, 2000.

ZAKOVITCH's *Introduction* is currently available only in Hebrew. In a context where Israeli academic biblical scholarship was largely governed by European models, it "translates" for that readership the more hermeneutical approaches of academic Jewish studies in North America, such as the work of FISHBANE and KUGEL. In addition, it provides valuable criteria for defining inner-biblical allusions and isolating interpretive activity. The article in the Haran Festschrift draws attention to a fascinating literary and exegetical phenomenon. Once a difficult legal text is interpreted or reinterpreted by another text, at a later stage, an editor may adjust the source text, by means of an interpolation, to make it consistent with the text that interprets it. He demonstrates this issue with a close examination of the laws for asylum in the case of unintentional homicide in the Covenant Code and Deuteronomy (Exod 21:13–14; Deut 19:11–12). Although in the abstract, this may sound at first like a mirror image being reflected back in another mirror to an infinite regress, the idea helps explain a number of issues in biblical law, where the texts comment upon one another. His short essay in English (2000) on the way that poetic texts served to catalyze the creation or enlargement of narrative passages in the Bible (and in postbiblical compositions) gives a good idea of the richness of Zakovitch's approach.

HAYS, Richard B. *Echoes of Scripture in the Literature of Paul.* New Haven, Conn.: Yale University Press, 1993.

This monograph sheds light on the quotations of and allusions to the Hebrew Bible found frequently in the Pauline corpus. HAYS's study raises an interesting methodological question about the possibility of establishing the presence of textual allusion, even in the absence of direct quotation or the use of an explicit citation formula. Implicitly, the work of Hays suggests that the model of inner-biblical exegesis provides a valuable tool for understanding the New Testament as a form of reinterpretation of Scripture.

Otto, Eckart. *Theologische Ethik des Alten Testaments.* Theologische Wissenschaft 3.2. Stuttgart: W. Kohlhammer, 1994.

———. "Aspects of Legal Reforms and Reformulations in Ancient Cuneiform and Israelite Law." Pages 160–96 in *Theory and Method in Biblical and Cuneiform Law: Revision, Interpolation and Development.* Edited by Bernard M. Levinson. JSOTSup 181. Sheffield: Sheffield Academic Press, 1994.

———. "Von der Gerichtsordnung zum Verfassungsentwurf: Deuteronomische Gestaltung und deuteronomistische Interpretation im 'Ämtergesetz' Dtn 16,18–18,22." Pages 142–55 in "*Wer ist wie du, HERR, unter den Göttern?": Studien zur Theologie und Religionsgeschichte Israels für Otto Kaiser.* Edited by Ingo Kottsieper et al. Göttingen: Vandenhoeck & Ruprecht, 1995.

———. "Biblische Rechtsgeschichte als Fortschreibungsgeschichte." *BO* 56 (1999): 5–14; republished without title, review of Bernard M. Levinson, *Deuteronomy and the Hermeneutics of Legal Innovation, ZABR* 5 (1999): 329–38.

———. "False Weights in the Scales of Biblical Justice? Different Views of Women from Patriarchal Hierarchy to Religious Equality in the Book of Deuteronomy." Pages 128–46 in *Gender and Law in the Hebrew Bible and the Ancient Near East.* Edited by Victor H. Matthews, Bernard M. Levinson, and Tikva Frymer-Kensky. JSOTSup 262. Sheffield: Sheffield Academic Press, 1998; repr., London: T. & T. Clark, 2004.

———. "Innerbiblische Exegese im Heiligkeitsgesetz Levitikus 17–26." Pages 125–96 in *Levitikus als Buch.* Edited by Heinz-Josef Fabry and Hans-Winfried Jüngling. BBB 119. Berlin: Philo, 1999.

———. *Das Deuteronomium: Politische Theologie und Rechtsreform in Juda und Assyrien.* BZAW 284. Berlin: de Gruyter, 1999.

———. *Das Deuteronomium im Pentateuch und Hexateuch: Studien zur Literaturgeschichte von Pentateuch und Hexateuch im Lichte des Deuteronomiumrahmens.* FAT 30. Tübingen: Mohr Siebeck, 2000.

———. *Max Webers Studien des Antiken Judentums.* Tübingen: Mohr Siebeck, 2002.

———. "The Pentateuch in Synchronical and Diachronical Perspective: Protorabbinic Scribal Erudition Mediating between Deuteronomy and the Priestly Code." Pages 14–35 in *Das Deuteronomium zwischen Pentateuch und Deuteronomistischem Geschichtswerk.* Edited by Eckart Otto and Reinhard Achenbach. FRLANT 206. Göttingen: Vandenhoeck & Ruprecht, 2004.

———. "Scribal Scholarship in the Formation of Torah and Prophets: A Postexilic Scribal Discourse between Priestly Scholarship and Literary Prophecy—The Example of the Book of Jeremiah and Its Relation to the Pentateuch." Pages 171–84 in *The Pentateuch as Torah: New Models for Understanding Its Promulgation and Acceptance.* Edited by Gary N. Knoppers and Bernard M. Levinson. Winona Lake, Ind.: Eisenbrauns, 2007.

Eckart Otto specializes in the reception history of cuneiform law and its impact upon biblical law. He has made five major contributions to the field of academic Biblical Studies: (1) He begins the reconstruction of the literary history of the Pentateuch with Deuteronomy, as the literary, historical, and theological center of the Torah; this point of departure contrasts significantly with alternative models of pentateuchal theory, which begin rather with Genesis and with narrative; (2) his work attempts to reorient standard approaches to contemporary European pentateuchal theory in light of both legal history and inner-biblical exegesis; (3) Otto is one of the few contemporary scholars seeking to offer an overall theory to account for the composition and literary development of both the Pentateuch and the Deuteronomistic History;[23] (4) he sees a continuity in literary, exegetical, and sociological terms between the tradents responsible for the Deuteronomistic History and the eventual emergence of the Pharisaic movement in the Second Temple period;[24] and finally (5) Otto argues that the legal and cultural system of ancient Israel is essential to the emergence of modernity. To make this argument, he draws upon his extensive work in sociological theory and on the scholarship of Max Weber.

The titles included here represent only a small portion of Otto's prolific output; the focus is especially on English publications to provide a sense of his range. Otto seeks to place contemporary European pentateuchal theory on a firm foundation, based upon his theory of the literary relationship of the various biblical legal collections. The article "Aspects of Legal Reforms and Reformulations in Ancient Cuneiform and Israelite Law" provides a good overview of his approach. Since his early development as a form critic trained in redaction criticism, Otto has embraced the model of inner-biblical exegesis. He finds the model helpful as a way to understand the composition of Deuteronomy, which he understands as a revision of the Covenant Code, and then also of the Holiness Code (Lev

23 See also, with a different approach, Reinhard G. KRATZ, *Die Komposition der erzählenden Bücher des Alten Testaments: Grundwissen der Bibelkritik* (UTB 2157; Göttingen: Vandenhoeck & Ruprecht 2000); translated as *The Composition of the Narrative Books of the Old Testament* (trans. John Bowden; London: T & T Clark, 2005).

24 A similar argument was made by VEIJOLA (see entry herein) concerning the emergence of scribalism as a distinct form of religious identity; Otto takes the argument further by positing the specific sociological tie to the Pharisaic movement.

17–26), which he regards as an exilic attempt to synthesize and integrate the Covenant Code, Deuteronomy, and priestly ideals into a unified and coherent system.

His study of theological ethics (1994) is written for a broader audience and provides an excellent overview of his basic orientation. He places special emphasis upon the role played by the legal texts as providing a set of ethical and religious norms. This approach counters the antinomianism he finds in Christian ethical theory and offers a sympathetic reading of the value system underlying biblical law. The stimulating monograph-length article on the Holiness Code (1999) advocates a model of exegesis as essential for understanding its composition. Distinctive here is the argument that the Holiness Code, in its redactional structure as well as in its contents, represents an interpretive rereading and integration of earlier biblical legal collections. He maintains that the Holiness Code represents a harmonization of Deuteronomy 12–26 with the Priestly source, with the Covenant Code functioning as a hermeneutical key to reading the new composition.

The view that legal history within the Bible should be understood in terms of the history of interpretation is developed further in "Biblische Rechtsgeschichte als Fortschreibungsgeschichte," which is a review essay of my *Deuteronomy and the Hermeneutics of Legal Innovation.* Here he argues that the model of inner-biblical exegesis provides a valuable new tool for standard source-critical approaches while equally emphasizing that inner-biblical exegesis should be informed by careful analysis of the literary layers of the text. Further, he challenges my argument that the authors of the legal corpus of Deuteronomy originally sought to contest the authority and status of the

Covenant Code and, instead, maintains that a model of exegesis requires a notion that Deuteronomy was intended merely as a supplement to the Covenant Code. Otto's approach seems to impose an anachronistic conception of canonical authority upon the biblical text and to read the preexilic text in light of its postexilic reception.[25] This is not the place to address these issues, but it is valuable to have the clear outline of the alternative possibilities of interpretation so clearly delineated.

A number of scholars have recently argued that the formation of the Pentateuch was the result of a historic compromise between priestly and nonpriestly lay perspectives.[26] Otto's innovative and suggestive "Scribal Scholarship in the Formation of Torah and Prophets: A Postexilic Scribal Discourse between Priestly Scholarship and Literary Prophecy—The Example of the Book of Jeremiah

[25] For the most recent analysis of this issue, see Jeffrey STACKERT, *Rewriting the Torah: Literary Revision in Deuteronomy and the Holiness Legislation* (FAT 52; Tübingen: Mohr Siebeck, 2007), 209–25 (on "Literary Dependence and Compositional Logic: Understanding the Motivation for Biblical Legal Revision"). Challenging Otto's argument that Deut 1:5 means that Deuteronomy understands itself as an exegetical supplement, Christophe NIHAN, *From Priestly Torah to Pentateuch: A Study in the Composition of the Book of Leviticus* (FAT 2/25; Tübingen: Mohr Siebeck, 2007), 553–54n614; and Joachim Schaper, "The 'Publication' of Legal Texts in Ancient Judah," in *The Pentateuch as Torah: New Models for Understanding Its Promulgation and Acceptance* (ed. Gary N. Knoppers and Bernard M. Levinson; Winona Lake, Ind.: Eisenbrauns, 2007), 225–35 (at 227–28).

[26] The position is most often associated with Erhard Blum, *Studien zur Komposition des Pentateuch* (BZAW 189; Berlin: de Gruyter, 1990). But see Morton Smith, "Pseudepigraphy in the Israelite Literary Tradition," in *Pseudepigrapha I: Pseudopythagorica, Lettres de Platon, Littérature pseudépigraphique juive* (ed. Kurt von Fritz; Entretiens sur l'antiquité classique 18; Vandoeuvres, Geneva: Fondation Hardt, 1972), 191–215 (with panel discussion, 216–27).

and Its Relation to the Pentateuch" argues against it.[27] He sees the Pentateuch as the result of a post-Priestly scribal effort to mediate between the Priestly work and a Deuteronomistic edition of Deuteronomy. In this process, the editors of the Pentateuch developed scribal techniques, which subsequently became the foundation for rabbinic interpretations and reapplications of Scripture. A critical part of Otto's overall argument is that the postexilic formations of the Pentateuch and the book of Jeremiah were each the result of intensive endeavors of scribes, who employed the same sorts of exegetical techniques. A second, equally critical part of the argument is that those priestly scribes responsible for the formation of the Pentateuch were avidly debating critical tenets of the nature and extent of revelation, as well as the hermeneutics of revelation, with scribes belonging to the postexilic prophetic schools. The implication of Otto's study is that the formation of the larger prophetic books, especially that of Jeremiah, influenced the formation of the Pentateuch, and vice versa. In this way, the Law and the Prophets do not appear as two diametrically opposed sets of literary works, separated from each other by genre, date, and content. They appear rather as two related sets of writings in conversation—or more often, heated debate—with each other about the meaning of biblical texts.

[27] The continuation of this paragraph closely follows Gary N. Knoppers and Bernard M. Levinson, "How, When, Where, and Why Did the Pentateuch Become the Torah?" in *The Pentateuch as Torah: New Models for Understanding Its Promulgation and Acceptance* (ed. Gary N. Knoppers and Bernard M. Levinson; Winona Lake, Ind.: Eisenbrauns, 2007), 1–19 (at 12–13).

LEVINSON, Bernard M. *Deuteronomy and the Hermeneutics of Legal Innovation.* New York: Oxford University Press, 1997.

———. "The Metamorphosis of Law into Gospel: Gerhard von Rad's Attempt to Reclaim the Old Testament for the Church" (coauthor: Douglas Dance). Pages 83–110 in *Recht und Ethik im Alten Testament.* Edited by Bernard M. Levinson and Eckart Otto, with assistance from Walter Dietrich. Münster: LIT Verlag, 2004.

———. "The Birth of the Lemma: The Restrictive Reinterpretation of the Covenant Code's Manumission Law by the Holiness Code (Leviticus 25:44–46)." *JBL* 124 (2005): 617–39.

———. *"The Right Chorale": Studies in Biblical Law and Interpretation.* FAT 54. Tübingen: Mohr Siebeck, 2008.

Deuteronomy and the Hermeneutics of Legal Innovation applies the model of inner-biblical exegesis to the legal corpus of Deuteronomy. Deuteronomy's authors introduced a radically new system of religious law that was viewed as essential for the nation's survival at the time of the Neo-Assyrian crisis. Seeking to defend this transformation of prevailing norms, the reformers turned to earlier laws found in the Covenant Code—even when those laws contradicted their own views—and revised them in such a way as to lend authority to their new understanding of divine will. Passages in the legal corpus long viewed as redundant or displaced represent the attempt by Deuteronomy's authors to sanction their legal vision before the legacy of the past. The attribution of an innovation to a tradition that is actually inconsistent with it represents a technique of authorship evident elsewhere in biblical and postbiblical literature and helps open up a broader view of Israelite and Jewish religious history. The Holiness Code (Lev 17–26) fits closely within this tradition, as demonstrated in "The Birth of the Lemma." This article argues that the rejection of the very idea of one Israelite being enslaved to another (Lev 25:39–46) represents a sustained revision and reinterpretation of the prior manumission laws of both the Covenant Code (Exod 21:2–11) and Deut 15:12–18. The Septuagint translator misunderstood the technical Hebrew formula involved and provided a different interpretation of it. That misunderstanding has had a lasting impact upon the unit's translation, while obscuring the power of the exegetical reworking. The article on Gerhard von Rad analyzes the alarming changes that took place in Germany during the period 1933–1945. It investigates the impact of the social location of the interpreter upon his or her way of reading and interpreting the biblical text. In this way, the study points to an issue not directly addressed in the present volume: the extent to which the concepts of both canon and exegesis are equally constructions of the historical present, not simply an inheritance of the past that the interpreter seeks to retrieve. "*The Right Chorale*" presents twelve selected investigations of textual composition, interpretation, revision, and transmission. Originally published over a decade and a half and significantly revised and updated, the studies explore the connections between law and narrative, show the connections between Deuteronomy and the Neo-Assyrian loyalty oath tradition, address the relationship of Deuteronomy and the Covenant Code, reflect upon questions of methodology, and explore the contributions of the Bible to later Western intellectual history. The unifying thread is the focus upon ancient hermeneutics and the application of such a model to new areas such as text criticism and the reception and reinterpretation of cuneiform literature in ancient Israel.

Sommer, Benjamin D. "Exegesis, Allusion and Intertextuality in the Hebrew Bible: A Response to Lyle Eslinger." *VT* 46 (1996): 479–89.

———. *A Prophet Reads Scripture: Allusion in Isaiah 40–66.* Contraversions: Jews and Other Differences. Stanford, Calif.: Stanford University Press, 1998.

———. "Revelation at Sinai in the Hebrew Bible and in Jewish Theology." *JR* 79 (1999): 422–51.

———. "Inner-biblical Interpretation." Pages 1829–35 in *The Jewish Study Bible.* Edited by Adele Berlin and Marc Zvi Brettler. Oxford: Oxford University Press, 2004.

Sommer's beautifully written book offers a new perspective on the author of Isaiah 40–66 as a reader and interpreter of Scripture. His approach breaks down some of the binary oppositions that endure in the discipline between prophecy (often imagined as oral and immediate) and textuality. He shows the extent to which the author of Isaiah 40–66 (which he regards as a unified literary composition) was "a reader of Scripture": that is, the extent to which prophecy was here a conscious literary activity, as new prophecies were created out of old ones. The first chapter of his book, which expands and revises the article from 1996, is especially valuable. Sommer develops clear criteria to distinguish current work in intertextuality, which is popular in many areas of contemporary literary theory, from allusion. The former he considers as reader oriented and synchronic; the latter, author oriented and diachronic. Only in the case of the latter—where there is clear evidence of an author alluding to and consciously reworking a source to make a new statement—can one speak meaningfully of inner-biblical exegesis. Building on the work of other scholars, Sommer offers four steps to identify this kind of allusion: (1) identifying a textual element or pattern that has its home in another, independent text; (2) identifying the source text that is being evoked; (3) identifying the specific techniques whereby that text has been modified; and (4) finding evidence that the source text is somehow being reactivated in the new context. Sommer then implements this approach by demonstrating the systematic nature of allusion in Isaiah 40–66. He systematically shows the extent to which Jeremiah functioned as a major literary source: judgment oracles are transformed into oracles of restoration; unfulfilled prophecies are repredicated; earlier prophecies are presented as fulfilled; and typological connections are made. Subsequent chapters demonstrate similar reuse of First Isaiah, Micah, Nahum, and Hosea, and then emphasize the consistency of the literary and exegetical techniques employed in the reworking of earlier prophetic oracles in the new context. At this point, however, a question should be raised. Does a common technique for reworking older oracles, which Sommer finds in Isaiah 40–66, necessarily point to a single author of these chapters, as Sommer assumes? Due consideration not only of the exegetical form but also of the content and message of the oracles leads in a different direction. More likely, as is widely held in biblical scholarship, there seem to have been two distinct anonymous prophets at work, each of whom was engaged with reanimating earlier prophetic tradition: Second Isaiah (chapters 40–55) and Trito-Isaiah (chapters 56–66). This reservation aside, Sommer's volume shows the importance of the model of inner-biblical exegesis for understanding Israelite prophecy. Sommer is also doing crucial work in the area of Jewish biblical theology. His analysis of the Sinai pericope in the article from 1999 is brilliant. Embodying an immense amount of research, he shows how Sinai, presented as a moment of origin, is already a sophisticated exegetical composition. Finally, his summary of inner-biblical exegesis for *The Jewish Study Bible* introduces the issues in a clear and concise way. The volume itself, with essays spanning the entire history of Jewish biblical interpretation (e.g., nonrabbinic, rabbinic, Kabbalah, medieval philosophy), is a gem.

SCHMID, Konrad. *Buchgestalten des Jeremiabuches: Untersuchungen zur Redaktions- und Rezeptionsgeschichte von Jer 30–33 im Kontext des Buches.* WMANT 72. Neukirchen-Vluyn: Neukirchener Verlag, 1996.

———. "Innerbiblische Schriftauslegung: Aspekte der Forschungsgeschichte." Pages 1–22 in *Schriftauslegung in der Schrift: Festschrift für Odil Hannes Steck zu seinem 65. Geburtstag.* Edited by Reinhard Gregor Kratz, Thomas Krüger, and Konrad Schmid. BZAW 300. Berlin; New York: de Gruyter, 2000.

Konrad SCHMID is a Swiss scholar associated primarily with two major areas of research: the recent ferment in pentateuchal theory, where he has contributed extensively (as did his father, who was one of the pioneers in the reevaluation of the Yahwist[28]), and inner-biblical exegesis.[29] The remarks here will be restricted to the latter dimension of

[28] Hans Heinrich Schmid, *Der sogenannte Jahwist: Beobachtungen und Fragen zur Pentateuchforschung* (Zürich: Theologischer Verlag, 1976).

[29] See his Habilitation, *Erzväter und Exodus: Untersuchungen zur doppelten Begründung der Ursprünge Israels in den Geschichtsbüchern des Alten Testaments* (WMANT 81; Neukirchen-Vluyn: Neukirchener Verlag, 1999); and Thomas B. Dozeman and Konrad Schmid, eds., *A Farewell to the Yahwist? The Composition of the Pentateuch in Recent European Interpretation* (SBLSymS 34; Atlanta: Society of Biblical Literature, 2006).

his work. While training with Odil Hannes Steck, he has now sought to bring that approach into dialogue with North American approaches to inner-biblical exegesis: to directly compare the various methodological assumptions and to apply that method to the prophetic corpus in particular. Schmid's volume on Jeremiah is fascinating for what it represents in the history of scholarship as much as for its particular arguments. It does seem to represent a genuine new approach to the compositional history of Jeremiah. Here it is no longer a matter of the conventional literary stratification designed to distinguish the original oral utterances of the prophet, the third-person Baruch narrative, and the prose sermons of the Deuteronomistic Historian. Instead, the goal is to investigate the formation of Jeremiah as a book. The focus shifts radically from the recovery of the words of an individual "behind" the book to the book itself as a literary and religious composition. He seeks to integrate European redaction criticism with more synchronic and literary readings.

Intellectual genealogy here provides interesting ways to read texts and approaches alongside one another. Just as Sommer's volume on Isaiah (just discussed) represents a new development of Fishbane's approach, applied to an extended corpus, so does Schmid represent a new application of the Steck model to the formation of Jeremiah, employing modern literary methods. The comparison of the two highlights the different conceptions of how to understand inner-biblical exegesis. Thematic comparisons are equally interesting. If Jean-Pierre Sonnet makes the formation of the ספר, "scroll" or "book," of Deuteronomy the key to understanding its plot and its allusions to other literature (see the following entry), so does Schmid here make the ספר the key to understanding the formation of Jeremiah as a book. Sonnet is more synchronic, drawing upon Meir Sternberg as a model; Schmid hews closer to the redactional-historical model of his *Doktorvater.* Just as Steck had argued that Isaiah 35 was composed as a *redaktionelle Brücke* [redactional bridge, or linchpin] to join First Isaiah (Isa 1–39) with Deutero-Isaiah (Isa 40–55), so does Schmid see Jeremiah 30–33 as playing a similar function. He sees the unit as having no prior independent circulation but as being composed as a coherent unit, with a distinctive use of the term ספר, "scroll," to integrate and unify the various redactions of the book of Jeremiah into a unified whole.

Schmid's article in the Steck Festschrift, "Innerbiblische Schriftauslegung: Aspekte der Forschungsgeschichte," reveals an impressive grasp of the history of scholarship and connects the emergence of the method to the standard methodologies in Biblical Studies, showing the impact of the newer approach in different fields of Biblical Studies. The article covers all the different genres and sections of the Bible: the narrative and legal material of the Pentateuch, including current pentateuchal theory; new approaches to the prophetic corpus; psalms and Hebrew poetry; and Chronicles. He shows how comparable questions arise in some of the different subspecializations of the discipline, without sufficiently being brought into conjunction. He also demonstrates the extent to which inner-biblical exegesis can itself function as a criterion for identifying diachronic development in a text. In this way, he seeks to expand the repertoire of the exegete, so that it is not only conventional literary criticism that is the foundation of all else. The one method is not somehow prior and more definitive than the other, as some scholars have claimed; each complements the other.

SONNET, Jean-Pierre. *The Book within the Book: Writing in Deuteronomy.* Biblical Interpretation 14. Leiden: E. J. Brill, 1997.

———. "'Lorsque Moïse eut achevé d'écrire . . .' (Dt 31,24). Une théorie narrative de l'écriture dans le Pentateuque." *RSR* 90 (2002): 509–24.

SONNET's work directly confronts the paradox that Deuteronomy offers a narrative of its own formation as a book while nonetheless presupposing that existence from the very beginning. In literary terms, the plot of the book is the creation of the book itself. The literary figure of Moses, depicted as a scribe in the story of Deuteronomy, permits the book's authors to legitimate their own work as authors, editors, and interpreters. Drawing on Near Eastern literature and integrating synchronic and diachronic perspectives, this sensitive analysis of Deuteronomy has been recognized as "ein Meilenstein in der Deuteronomiumforschung" [a milestone in Deuteronomy scholarship].[30]

BAR-ON [Gesundheit], Shimon. "The Festival Calendars in Exodus XXIII 14–19 and XXXIV 18–26." *VT* 48 (1998): 161–95.

[30] Thus Eckart OTTO, "Mose der Schreiber: Zu 'poetics' und 'genetics' in der Deuteronomiumsanalyse anhand eines Buches von Jean-Pierre Sonnet," *ZABR* 6 (2000): 320–29 (at 329); and published in idem, *Gottes Recht als Menschenrecht: Rechts- und literaturhistorische Studien sum Deuteronomium* (BZAR 2; Wiesbaden: Harrassowitz, 2002), 84–91. Note also the assessment provided by Timo VEIJOLA, describing the important contributions of narrative approaches to the historical-critical analysis of Deuteronomy ("Deuteronomismusforschung zwischen Tradition und Innovation," *TRu* 67 [2002]: 273–327).

———. "Intertextualität und literarhistorische Analyse der Festkalender in Exodus und im Deuteronomium." Pages 190–220 in *Festtraditionen in Israel und im Alten Orient*. VWGTh 28. Edited by Erhard Blum and Rüdiger Lux. Gütersloh: Gütersloher Verlagshaus, 2006.

The two articles cited by GESUNDHEIT (one published under the Hebrew name BAR-ON) are studies prepared in the course of revising his dissertation for publication as a major two-volume study on the festival calendar in ancient Israel, which will appear in the series FAT. The eagerly awaited work promises to be a major contribution to the field, given the author's superb grasp of the history of scholarship, from the classical source-critical studies of the nineteenth century through to contemporary pentateuchal theory. The first article breaks new ground by raising the question of models, assumptions, and methodology. The legal revelation in Exodus 34 has conventionally been viewed as an ancient legal source, one of the very oldest in the Bible, dating to the early settlement period.[31] This article challenges that approach. Although other studies have also argued for the text's late composition, this article uses a different approach and demonstrates how Exodus 34 systematically reinterprets older legal material from a range of different literary sources. The author shows how inner-biblical exegesis helps account for the key features and composition of this text. Although questions may be asked about the author's hesitation to consider material from Deuteronomy as relevant to his analysis of

[31] See Bernard M. Levinson, "Goethe's Analysis of Exodus 34 and Its Influence on Julius Wellhausen: The *Pfropfung* of the Documentary Hypothesis," *ZAW* 114 (2002): 212–23.

the literary history, the article makes essential reading for any new understanding of Exodus 34. The second article offers an important study of Deuteronomy's presentation of the Passover (Deut 16:1–8), comparing and contrasting the contributions of inner-biblical exegesis and classical redaction criticism. Because a proper understanding of the history of the Passover is essential to any broader analysis of the history of Israelite literature and religion, this study warrants careful attention. The author is more confident than I am of the possibility of constructing a detailed redactional history of the unit, but he shares my basic position that Deuteronomy's Passover can only be understood in terms of inner-biblical legal exegesis.

Ska, Jean Louis. *Introduction to Reading the Pentateuch.* Translated by Sr. Pascale Dominique. Winona Lake, Ind: Eisenbrauns, 2006. This volume is a translation, with extensive new material added, of *Introduction à la lecture du Pentateuque: Clés pour l'interprétation des cinq premiers livres de la Bible.* Le livre et le rouleau 5. Brussels: Éditions Lessius, 2000.

Among recent introductions to the Pentateuch, that of Jean Louis Ska distinguishes itself with its careful attention to the Bible as a written text. The volume begins with an examination of the individual books of the Pentateuch in their present form as a way of introducing the reader to larger questions of composition and redaction. Particular focus is placed upon the legal corpora and the interpretive issues they raise, including the question of their literary sequence and relation and the presence of interpolations and editorial devices. The volume offers a first-rate introduction to the most recent European theories (including the attempt to redate the Yahwist as a late author and the increasing focus upon post-Priestly redactional activity), where the author himself has made extensive contributions. With its focus upon the essential role of editors and the techniques they employ, the model of revision and rewriting as a distinctive form of authorship in the Bible remains at the center of Ska's attention. The volume is also important for its larger vision of the discipline: Ska frequently makes astute connections between the history of biblical scholarship and broader cultural and intellectual history in a way that is seldom seen in more conventional biblical scholarship.

BRETTLER, Marc Z. "'A Literary Sermon' in Deuteronomy 4." Pages 33–50 in *"A Wise and Discerning Mind": Essays in Honor of Burke O. Long*. Edited by Saul M. Olyan and Robert C. Culley. BJS 325. Providence, R.I.: Brown Judaic Studies, 2000.

The short article by BRETTLER provides an opportunity to rethink the standard way of looking at Deuteronomy as a series of sermons by countryside Levites, a position long advocated by Gerhard von Rad and one that found widespread acceptance. Brettler shows the history of that idea and the extent to which it fails to explain the evidence. His excellent analysis then turns to the text of Deuteronomy itself and examines chapter 4, the long sermon on monotheism, to show how this text represents a literary composition and the extent to which only a model of exegesis can provide a satisfactory explanation for the text. Other work by Brettler (cited in the article) makes a similar argument for Deuteronomy 30.

WEVERS, John W. *Notes on the Greek Text of Deuteronomy*. SBLSCS 39. Atlanta: Scholars Press, 1995.

———. "The Interpretative Character and Significance of the Septuagint Version." Pages 84–107 in *Hebrew Bible/ Old Testament: The History of Its Interpretation*, vol. 1: *From the Beginnings to the Middle Ages (until 1300)*. Part 1: *Antiquity*. Edited by Magne Sæbø. Göttingen: Vandenhoeck & Ruprecht, 1996).

DOGNIEZ, Cécile, and Marguerite HARL, eds. *Le Pentateuque d'Alexandrie: La Bible des Septante, texte grec et traduction*. La Bible d'Alexandrie. Paris: Éditions du Cerf, 2001.

PIETERSMA, Albert, and Benjamin G. WRIGHT, eds. *A New English Translation of the Septuagint*. New York: Oxford University Press, 2007. Online: http://ccat.sas.upenn.edu/nets; cited March 20, 2008.

KRAUS, Wolfgang, and Martin KARRER, eds. *Septuaginta Deutsch*, vol. 1: *Das griechische Alte Testament in deutscher Übersetzung*. Stuttgart: Deutsche Bibelgesellschaft, 2008.

The Greek translation of the Hebrew Bible, the Septuagint, was prepared for the thriving Jewish community at Alexandria, Egypt, circa 225 B.C.E. The Septuagint version also provides the earliest independent example of the interpretation of the Bible. The translators sought to explain difficult words, to reconcile inconsistent laws, and to make the ancient text of the Pentateuch "present" and relevant to their situation. The Septuagint therefore bears a fascinating relation to its Hebrew parent text (which does not necessarily correspond to the present Masoretic text). In many cases, the Septuagint preserves a witness to earlier religious ideas in the biblical text that were subsequently "corrected" to bring it into conformity with later Jewish monotheism (as in the case of the clear recognition of Yahweh's ruling over a divine council or pantheon at Deut 32:8 and 32:43). Elsewhere, the reverse holds true. In translating the Hebrew Scriptures into their living language of Greek, the community at Alexandria saw the Torah as also telling their own story and addressing them in the present.

For example, the Hebrew text of Deuteronomy threatens "you will become an object of horror (והיית לזעוה) for all the kingdoms of the earth" (Deut 28:25). This treaty curse alludes to the destruction brought about by the Babylonian invasion and exile of Judah in 587 B.C.E., construed as punishment for national wrongdoing. The translator of the Septuagint reinterprets that punishment as an allusion to the community in Alexandria: "and you will become a dispersion (καὶ ἔσῃ ἐν διασπορᾷ) among the kingdoms of the earth" (WEVERS, *Greek Text of Deuteronomy*, 437–38). The contemporary situation of *diaspora* is read back into the biblical text. Accordingly, each divergence between the Hebrew (MT) text and that of the Septuagint and other versions must be decided on a case-by-case basis, to assess which offers the better reading. Perhaps more important, the Septuagint should be seen not simply as a text-critical tool but as a witness to the ongoing life of biblical interpretation in the Second Temple period.

A resurgence of interest in the Septuagint has led to important new translation and commentary projects in English, French, and German. *A New English Translation of the Septuagint* (NETS) has just been published; NETS has also placed valuable resources online. An excellent window into the world of the Septuagint is the translation, commentary, and critical apparatus provided in the French series, La Bible d'Alexandrie. The volume *Le Pentateuque d'Alexandrie* brings together the earlier, separately published volumes on the Pentateuch and updates and corrects them to ensure consistency of translation. The Greek and French texts are published on facing pages. As the editors themselves acknowledge in several cases (e.g., Deuteronomy), it would have been better to employ the critical Greek text prepared by John W. WEVERS[32] for the Göttingen Septuagint rather than the older edition by Alfred Rahlfs.[33] At particular points where the editors thought it relevant, however, the reading by Wevers was cited. Wevers has also provided his larger perspective on the Septuagint in his article, "The Interpretative Character and Significance of the Septuagint Version." Distinguishing his approach is the assumption that the Septuagint of Deuteronomy was an interpretation, and not simply a direct translation, of the underlying Hebrew. Finally, the first publication of the major German translation and commentary project, *Septuaginta Deutsch*, is scheduled for 2008.

Tov, Emanuel. *Textual Criticism of the Hebrew Bible.* 2d rev. ed. Minneapolis: Augsburg Fortress; Assen: Royal Van Gorcum, 2001.

———. *Scribal Practices and Approaches Reflected in the Texts Found in the Judean Desert.* STDJ 54. Leiden: E. J. Brill, 2004.

No evidence is more compelling for the role of scribes in the creation of the Bible than the biblical text itself: that is, the plurality of its textual witnesses, with all the

32 See John W. Wevers, *Deuteronomium* (Septuaginta: Vetus Testamentum graecum auctoritate academiae scientiarum gottingensis editum 3.2; Göttingen: Vandenhoeck & Ruprecht, 1977).

33 The original 1935 edition of the Septuagint was not fully critical and presented an eclectic text, drawing upon several different manuscript traditions. Under the auspices of the German Bible Society, which has taken an international leadership role in making such resources available, an extensively revised and corrected edition has been published that offers the best single volume edition of the Septuagint. See Alfred Rahlfs and Robert Hanhart, *Septuaginta: id est Vetus Testamentum graece iuxta LXX interpretes, editio altera* (2 vols. in 1; 2d ed; Stuttgart: Deutsche Bibelgesellschaft, 2006).

light that they shed upon inevitable errors of transmission, confusion of letters, scribal errors, annotations and intentional theological changes or "corrections," variant textual traditions, multiple recensions of the same tradition, and different "editions" of the same biblical book. Emanuel Tov has devoted a professional lifetime to tracing the details of the formation of the biblical text, drawing upon the significance of the Septuagint and the evidence of the Dead Sea Scrolls in particular. In *Textual Criticism of the Hebrew Bible*, he offers a detailed introduction to the textual witnesses of the Bible (Hebrew, Samaritan, Septuagint, Dead Sea Scrolls, and epigraphic evidence). He develops helpful criteria to distinguish between the roles of author and scribe in the composition, redaction, and transmission of the biblical text. In his extensive treatment of the role of harmonization (as in the proto-Samaritan textual witness preserved at Qumran) he demonstrates how, at an early point, scribes were very much aware of the existence of divergent traditions within the biblical text and often sought to eliminate inconsistencies by exegetically aligning one text with another. This kind of objectively tracked evidence can, in turn, provide a heuristic model for the composition of the biblical text itself. Remarkably, Tov acknowledges "text plurality" as having been the rule up until the end of the first century C.E. He concludes that it was less a matter of the triumph of the text itself (as if the MT were somehow intrinsically a better text) than the triumph of this text's Pharisaic supporters as the dominant organized Jewish group who survived the destruction of the Second Temple in 70 C.E. (194–95). Tov's *Scribal Practices* provides an exhaustive introduction to the realia—the nitty-gritty—of the tools and techniques used by ancient scribes: the material, shape, and preparation of the scrolls; ink and writing implements; scripts and writing conventions; errors and their correction; scribal signs; and the possible existence of scribal schools, such as that at Qumran. Accompanied by extensive illustrations and charts of scribal signs, the volume provides a window into the importance of scribal traditions and training in ancient Israel.

CARR, David M. "Method in Determination of Direction of Dependence: An Empirical Test of Criteria Applied to Exodus 34,11–26 and Its Parallels." Pages 107–40 in *Gottes Volk am Sinai.* Edited by Matthias Köckert and Erhard Blum. VWGTh 18. Gütersloh: Gütersloher Verlag, 2001.

———. *Writing on the Tablet of the Heart: Origins of Scripture and Literature.* New York: Oxford University Press, 2005.

VAN SETERS, John. "The Origins of the Hebrew Bible: Some New Answers to Old Questions, Part Two" (review essay of David M. Carr, *Writing on the Tablets of the Tablets of the Heart: The Origins of Scripture and Literature*). *Journal of Ancient Near Eastern Religions* 7 (2007): 219–37.

CARR uses Exodus 34, whose relationship to its legal and literary parallels is hotly disputed, as a test case to develop general criteria for determining the direction of literary dependence in cases of parallel texts. The difficulty of establishing "earlier than" or "later than" is thus the focus of this article. It provides a methodological advance by considering literature from the Dead Sea Scrolls, where there is clear dependence on biblical material, to provide empirical examples. He considers the Temple Scroll (11QTemple), the "Reworked Pentateuch" (4QRP or 4Q365), and the proto-Samaritan text (4QpaleoExod^{m}). This article valuably helps isolate techniques of exegetical reworking and criteria for establishing the direction of literary dependence in cases of inner-biblical exegesis. In the work published in 2005, building on a key proposal of André LEMAIRE, Carr makes an ambitious, cross-cultural argument. He maintains that ancient societies cultivated elites of young males whose training for positions of social and political leadership demanded mastery of a curriculum of arcane texts. Mastery of this curriculum, which was often written in a remote language and/or script, involved both oral memorization and written transcription. In that way, the model seeks to overcome the standard dichotomy between orality and literacy. Carr's study is informed by a wide range of material from ancient Egypt, Sumero-Akkadian literature, classical *paideia*, and comparative religion. What seems unclear, however, is whether the notion of curriculum suffices to explain either the delimited corpus of scripture or the broad range of instructional literature in the Second Temple period (as noted by Van Seters in his careful review essay).

SCORALICK, Ruth. *Gottes Güte und Gottes Zorn: Die Gottesprädikationen in Exodus 34,6f und ihre intertextuellen Beziehungen zum Zwölfprophetenbuch.* HBS 33. Freiburg: Herder, 2002.

SCORALICK provides a canonical-intertextual reading of the divine attribute formula of Exodus 34:6–7, examining its role in the chapter and in the broader context of Exodus 32–34. She then investigates its connection to various texts in the twelve minor prophets (e.g., Hos 1:2–2:3, 11, 14:2–9, and Joel 2:1–14). The proclamation of the divine attributes in Exodus 34:6–7, in the context of the narrative of the breach and renewal of the covenant in Exodus 32–34, here becomes as a *Schlüsseltext* [key text] for understanding the overall coherence of the twelve minor prophets and their literary sequence (204). The volume is valuable for the basic questions of methodology that it raises. Scoralick's focus is not with inner-biblical exegesis but with intertextuality, to use the helpful distinction proposed by SOMMER. The analysis operates on a synchronic level: the texts are investigated in their present context in the canon. Although often rich in the reading of individual texts, the overall thesis becomes a bit difficult to follow. Diachronic conclusions seem to be drawn on the basis of a synchronic analysis of the evidence. When conducting a synchronic reading of the texts, it becomes unclear, for example, what it means to speak of the reception of the divine attributes in the Twelve, which would seem to assume a diachronic model. For example, does Hosea 1 have a relationship of textual dependence on Exodus 34:6–7, which can be linguistically demonstrated, or are the connections between the two passages nontextual and instead associative, general, and thematic (the concept of divine mercy)?

The approach of canonical reading departs from both standard source-critical or redaction-historical models and from the model of inner-biblical exegesis. It is no longer interested in attempting to demonstrate the literary dependence of one text on another, so as to show exegetical revision (the Fishbane model) or to use diachronic analysis to show how the redactional structure of a book reflects the reception and reinterpretation of earlier literary motifs (the Steck model). The focus shifts to a different horizon, presupposing the completion of the texts in their present shape, and finds strategies to make thematic, literary, and theological connections to integrate the disparate material.

NAJMAN, Hindy. *Seconding Sinai: The Development of Mosaic Discourse in Second Temple Judaism*. Supplements to the Journal for the Study of Judaism 77. Leiden: E. J. Brill, 2003.

NAJMAN seeks to reflect on the nature of the reuse and reinterpretation of Torah in postbiblical literature (Temple Scroll, Jubilees, Philo, and early rabbinic literature) and how this material develops a distinctive Mosaic discourse. She extends the analysis also into biblical material, addressing Deuteronomy and arguing against a notion of exegesis as entailing a challenge to the authority of the interpreted text. She maintains that Deuteronomy represents a continuation of Mosaic discourse that seeks to preserve earlier traditions faithfully as an authentic exposition of those traditions. The laws of Deuteronomy do not seek to compete with and replace but to supplement and exist alongside those of the Covenant Code. Her argument provides a valuable alternative approach to the one I advocated in *Deuteronomy and the Hermeneutics of Legal Innovation* and should be considered in the analysis of any case of exegesis. This is not the place to address the issues in the depth that they warrant. Her analysis of the postbiblical material, with the goal of creating a dialogue between First Temple and Second Temple exegetical literature, is very rich. However, by emphasizing the continuity between rewritten texts and their ancient sources rather than forms of discontinuity involved in rewriting, Najman seems to impose a postbiblical model, seeking harmonization, upon an ancient literature consisting of pluralistic and conflicting materials.[34]

34 See the detailed analysis by STACKERT (next entry), 211–14 and 221–22: "because the main focus of her study is interpretation in the

STACKERT, Jeffrey. *Rewriting the Torah: Literary Revision in Deuteronomy and the Holiness Legislation.* FAT 52. Tübingen: Mohr Siebeck, 2007.

STACKERT sheds important light on the legal material of the Holiness Code (hereafter in this section, H, or Lev 17–26, as well as significant parts of the priestly source elsewhere in the Pentateuch). He provides a systematic rethinking of the question of how to understand the relation of H to Deuteronomy (hereafter in this section, D): is there dependence and, if so, in which direction does it run? He selects four test cases where laws of similar content are found in the Covenant Code (Exod 21–23), D, and H: the laws of asylum, sabbatical, manumission of slaves, and tithes. With careful attention to language, legal sequence, and formulation, he argues that H depends upon both D and the Covenant Code. Equally important, he accounts for divergences of content and formulation, stressing the extent to which H redrafted and rethought its literary sources to meet new ideological goals. This

Temple Scroll, Jubilees, Philo, and early rabbinic literature, Najman overlooks the fact that the constraints of canonization that already exert a powerful influence over the perception and interpretation of the Bible in the post-biblical texts she examines are not operable for Deuteronomy [as a pre-exilic text]" (213). Similarly, as Maxine L. Grossmann notes: "Discourses construct realities, and contrasting discourses (especially those asserting the 'true meaning' of scripture) must be understood as having at least the potential to reflect interpretive competition and religious discord. Najman would have us understand rewritten scripture as a complement to its earlier source-texts. I would argue . . . that the claims of any given example of rewritten scripture must be seen in competition with others present in the same time and place" ("Beyond the Hand of Moses: Discourse and Interpretive Authority," *Proof* 26 [2006]: 294–301 [at 300]).

attention to the rationale and significance of the literary reuse and reworking makes Stackert's work distinctive. His work moves the model of inner-biblical exegesis forward by demonstrating the extent to which exegesis can entail profound reworking and domination of the literary source to a new goal. The last chapter of the volume is titled "Literary Dependence and Compositional Logic: Understanding the Motivation for Biblical Legal Revision" (209–25). Stackert here offers an incisive examination of the two contrasting models (supplement versus replacement) that have been proposed in recent scholarship to account for the relationship of both D and H to their textual sources, and he advocates the replacement model as providing the best explanation of the evidence. The Holiness Code, in his well-argued analysis, both synthesizes and supercedes previous legal collections within the Pentateuch. The volume closes with a rich discussion of various approaches to canon in religious studies and comparative literature.

NIHAN, Christophe. *From Priestly Torah to Pentateuch: A Study in the Composition of the Book of Leviticus*. FAT 2/25. Tübingen: Mohr Siebeck, 2007.

Christophe NIHAN recently completed this engaging and well-written dissertation. Although he and Stackert worked completely independently of one another, both are opening up new perspectives on the composition of the Pentateuch through their detailed analysis of narrative and legal material in Leviticus. Nihan's volume provides a new perspective on the composition of the Holiness Code by demonstrating the extent to which its author intended it from the beginning to respond to the other biblical legal collections and narrative sources. He provides a rich new way to think about the Holiness Code—so often viewed as a static work of fossilized ritual law—as a creative literary and exegetical composition. He integrates conventional redaction criticism with ritual studies, on the one hand, and the methodology of inner-biblical exegesis on the other. He dates Leviticus 1–16 to the Persian period under Darius I, and regards Leviticus 17–26 (27), as a later attempt to integrate the legislation of Deuteronomy with that of the Covenant Code (Exod 21–23). He stresses that interpretation was central to the composition of the Holiness Code and to understanding its function within the Second Temple period:

> [T]he composition of H participates . . . in the elaboration of the complex *hermeneutics of revelation* unifying the different prescriptions contained in the Torah. . . .
>
> . . . [T]he introduction of H at a strategic place within the Torah (namely between Ex 20–24 and D) may be viewed as laying out the *hermeneutical program* for reading (and learning) the entire Torah. (553, 555–56, italics in original)

Nihan's work makes inner-biblical exegesis central to understanding both Leviticus and the history of the composition of the Pentateuch.

ZAHN, Molly M. "Schneiderei oder Weberei? Zum Verständnis der Diachronie der Tempelrolle." *RevQ* 20 (2001): 255–86.

———. "Reexamining Empirical Models: The Case of Exodus 13." Pages 36–55 in *Das Deuteronomium zwischen Pentateuch und Deuteronomistischem Geschichtswerk.* Edited by Eckart Otto and Reinhard Achenbach. FRLANT 206. Göttingen: Vandenhoeck & Ruprecht, 2004.

———. "New Voices, Ancient Words: The *Temple Scroll's* Reuse of the Bible." Pages 435–58 in *Temple and Worship in Biblical Israel.* Edited by John Day. Library of Hebrew Bible/Old

Testament Studies 422. London: T & T Clark International, 2005.

ZAHN has written three studies that extend the method of inner-biblical exegesis to new areas. Her German article on the Temple Scroll (11QTemple) from Qumran single-handedly shows the deficit of the standard source-critical model that has been uncritically applied to that text. She demonstrates that it is essential to employ a hermeneutical model instead. Her article on Exodus 13 resolves a problem on whether this chapter is proto-Deuteronomic or Deuteronomistic by exploding that false alternative. Building on recent scholarship,[35] she demonstrates this chapter is a hermeneutical composition that draws upon a range of other biblical texts. The chapter is a late composition that derives, she argues, from the period that the various sources of the Pentateuch were being brought together. It represents an attempt to reconcile the different documents' inconsistent regulations. "Exodus 13 . . . creates a new version of the laws for Mazzot and Firstlings that aims to integrate the language and outlook of the various earlier laws" (54). Drawing upon methodological models more current in the study of Second Temple literature and the Dead Sea Scrolls, she demonstrates how the exegetical solution to the problem of inconsistent laws in the formative Pentateuch "is presented as God's original command" (54). The fascinating intellectual model here is that the process of formation of the Pentateuch already gave rise to attempts to harmonize and reconcile its various systems of

[35] In particular, Jan Christian Gertz, *Tradition und Redaktion in der Exoduserzählung: Untersuchungen zur Endredaktion des Pentateuch* (FRLANT 186; Göttingen: Vandenhoeck & Ruprecht, 2000).

legislation (Deuteronomy, the Covenant Code, the Priestly material). The 2005 article looks at the Temple Scroll from Qumran and how it reinterprets the biblical text, where the striking thing is "the Scroll's denial of its interpretive status, and its claim instead to represent the direct word of God" (435). She demonstrates how the attribution of the Temple Scroll to divine revelation has an impact upon how it interprets and reuses the biblical text. Her careful attention to the role of textual voice in creating an authority claim makes fascinating reading and has clear implications for the study of inner-biblical exegesis.

SCHAPER, Joachim. "Rereading the Law: Inner-Biblical Exegesis of Divine Oracles in Ezekiel 44 and Isaiah 56." Pages 125–44 in *Recht und Ethik im Alten Testament.* Edited by Bernard M. Levinson and Eckart Otto, with assistance from Walter Dietrich. ATM 13. Münster/London: LIT Verlag, 2004.

With an extended analysis of Second Isaiah's and Ezekiel's mutually exclusive reinterpretations of the same cluster of pentateuchal texts, SCHAPER emphasizes a phenomenon that becomes increasingly common in the Second Temple period: exegesis as a form of establishing community boundaries. The voicing of such interpretation as prophetic, while it is also clearly scribal and technical, is also significant. The recognition of such *schriftgelehrte Prophetie* [scribal prophecy] is a particularly valuable contribution of European approaches, and it breaks down the dichotomy that has long existed between prophecy and textualization. The essay closes with a valuable assessment of different models of exegesis and their explanatory power. Schaper's article, discussed earlier in the volume, addresses a series of issues that make it important for further work on inner-biblical exegesis. He draws together, compares, and valuably contrasts two different methodological models: (1) the extensive work of Fishbane on how two different Second Temple prophetic texts each reinterpret Deuteronomy's law regarding the exclusion of foreigners from the community; and (2) the approach of Odil Hannes STECK, which regards the entirety of Trito-Isaiah as an exegetical composition or redactional *Fortschreibung*. In the latter section of his fine article, he once again directly engages different intellectual models for conceptualizing the literary history of ancient Israel and shows how "inner-biblical exegesis [may serve as] a counter-weight to a *Literarkritik* [literary, or source criticism] that would otherwise become arbitrary and sterile" (143).

SCHNIEDEWIND, William M. *How the Bible Became a Book: The Textualization of Ancient Israel.* Cambridge: Cambridge University Press, 2004.

The emergence of a literature culture in ancient Israel provides the focus for SCHNIEDEWIND's book, which is written for a broad audience. It integrates a wide range of archaeological, epigraphic, and textual perspectives, and it maintains that ancient Israel became a literate society significantly before the conventional dating of literacy to Greece in the fifth century B.C.E. The synthetic approach is a real contribution. The author has published on a wide range of subjects elsewhere (epigraphy, archaeology, historical linguistics of classical and Qumran Hebrew), and this volume integrates those perspectives to provide an argument for the formation of the Pentateuch. Some aspects are open to question, including the author's setting the Priestly corpus and the Holiness Code (Lev 17–26) prior to Deuteronomy, and regarding the composition of the Pentateuch as essentially complete in the preexilic period. More significant is the assumption that, because a text employs a rhetoric that is oral (as in wisdom literature or the priestly material with its oral commands), it is therefore pre-textual and pre-literary. Even if a "book" is not explicitly present within the textual discourse, that need not imply a culture of orality. The system of ritual instructions, superscriptions, and colophons in the Priestly corpus shows all the signs of advanced scribal training. Moreover, an author may employ orality as an intentional literary strategy. Still, this work brings together a wealth of material not easily available elsewhere.[36]

VEIJOLA, Timo. "Die Deuteronomisten als Vorgänger der Schriftgelehrten: Ein Beitrag zur Entstehung des Judentums." Pages 192–240 in *Moses Erben: Studien zum Dekalog, zum Deuteronomismus und zum Schriftgelehrtentum.* BWA(N)T 149. Stuttgart: W. Kohlhammer, 2000.

———. "The Deuteronomistic Roots of Judaism." Pages 459–78 in *Sefer Moshe: The Moshe Weinfeld Jubilee Volume. Studies in the Bible and the Ancient Near East, Qumran, and Post-Biblical Judaism.* Edited by Chaim Cohen, Avi Hurvitz, and Shalom M. Paul. Winona Lake, Ind.: Eisenbrauns, 2004.

36 Some review essays include David M. Carr, Tamara C. Eskenazi, C. Mitchell, William M. Schniedewind, and Gary N. Knoppers, eds., *In Conversation with W. M. Schniedewind, "How the Bible Became A Book,"* special issue of *JHS* 5 (2004–5): article 18, http://www.arts.ualberta.ca/JHS/Articles/article_48.htm; cited September 20, 2007. See also the insightful, if unnecessarily sharply worded analysis by John Van Seters, "The Origins of the Hebrew Bible: Some New Answers to Old Questions," *Journal of Ancient Near Eastern Religions* 7 (2007): 87–108.

VEIJOLA shows the extent to which Deuteronomy can be understood only as the product of a literary sophistication that is more frequently associated with the late Second Temple period. He stresses the extent to which the religious significance of Deuteronomy, with its conceptions of covenant and prophecy, already reflect scribal thought. With this attentive analysis, he seeks to transform the way that Bible scholars have often understood the phenomenon of scribalism. He demonstrates the religious and literary creativity of scribal activity. Using this important perspective, he is also able to cast a new light on the emergence of rabbinic Judaism. Veijola argues that the scribal school responsible for the latest layers of Deuteronomy and of the Deuteronomistic History (the so-called nomistic redaction, or DtrN) leads directly to the kind of sophisticated scribal activity associated with "Ezra the priest-scribe, a scholar in matters concerning the commandments of YHWH and His laws in Israel" (see Ezra 7:11–12, NJPS). From there, it is but a short step, Veijola suggests, to Pharisaic (rabbinic) Judaism, with its focus on the scribal exegesis of Torah. Although there are a number of historical questions that could be asked, the larger challenge that Veijola poses to long-standing assumptions in the history of scholarship should not be overlooked. At issue is a rethinking of categories. This Finnish scholar, who died prematurely in 2005, seeks to challenge the standard dichotomy between preexilic and postexilic, between the religion of Israel and that of rabbinic Judaism, between the allegedly creative phase of the classical religion and the assumed decline into scribal legalism. Veijola rejects this kind of bifurcation in favor of a single, organic process, with Deuteronomy serving as the bridge.

APPROACHES TO EXEGESIS IN 1–2 CHRONICLES

Bendavid, Abba. *Maqbilot baMiqra* [Parallels in the Bible]. Jerusalem: Carta, 1972 (Hebrew).

Brettler, Marc Zvi. *The Creation of History in Ancient Israel.* London: Routledge, 1995.

Endres, John C., S. J., William R. Millar, and John Barclay Burns, eds. *Chronicles and Its Synoptic Parallels in Samuel, Kings, and Related Biblical Texts.* Collegeville, Minn.: Glazier/Liturgical, 1998.

Japhet, Sara. *The Ideology of the Book of Chronicles and Its Place in Biblical Thought.* BEATAJ 9. Frankfurt: Peter Lang, 1989.

———. *I & II Chronicles: A Commentary.* OTL. Louisville, Ky.: Westminster/John Knox, 1993.

Jonker, Louis. "Reforming History: The Hermeneutical Significance of the Books of Chronicles." *VT* 57 (2007): 21–44.

Kalimi, Isaac. *The Reshaping of Ancient Israelite History in Chronicles.* Winona Lake, Ind: Eisenbrauns, 2005.

Klein, Ralph W. *1 Chronicles: A Commentary.* Hermeneia; Minneapolis: Fortress, 2006.

Knoppers, Gary N. *1 Chronicles 1–9: A New Translation with Introduction and Commentary.* AB 12. New York: Doubleday, 2004.

———. *1 Chronicles 10–29: A New Translation with Introduction and Commentary.* AB 12A. New York: Doubleday, 2004.

Willi, Thomas. *Die Chronik als Auslegung: Untersuchungen zur literarischen Gestaltung der historischen Überlieferung Israels.* FRLANT 106. Göttingen: Vandenhoeck & Ruprecht, 1972.

The Chronicler employs a range of exegetical techniques to revise, expand, and update its literary sources. For that reason, Willi made exegesis the major template for understanding Chronicles, arguing that there was a need to adapt preexilic sources like the Deuteronomistic History to the situation in Persian period Yehud. Many scholars have questioned this approach as anachronistic in assuming the canonical or authoritative status of the Deuteronomistic History. The case of Chronicles is indeed complicated. At every point where Chronicles differs from the Deuteronomistic History, multiple factors must be taken into account before making any decision as to whether exegetical activity has taken place or whether other factors account for the differences. Some of these factors include textual criticism (at a given point, is Chronicles revising its source or simply working with a textual *Vorlage* that differs from what has been preserved in the MT?) and historiography (does the Chronicler have access to different historical sources than those that were available to the Deuteronomistic Historian and thereby differ from the latter in its presentation, or do the differences arise from exegetical transformation?).[37]

Chronicles also raises the question of the intent of its textual reworking: whether it serves simply to supplement and complement its sources, as its name in the Septuagint version would suggest—*Paraleipomêna*, that is, "things omitted" or "supplements"—where it follows 1–2 Samuel and 1–2 Kings. Marc Zvi BRETTLER adopts such a position: "the Chronicler was most likely not writing a history to replace Samuel and Kings, but desired to reshape the way in which these books would be read and remembered. . . . He attempted to supplement them" (22). This approach seems to me to view the Chronicler as the literary equivalent of a museum curator who took an antiquarian interest in the

[37] An additional methodological question, of course, involves the direction of literary dependence and, indeed, whether there is direct dependence of the Chronicler upon the Deuteronomistic History. The proposal by A. Graeme Auld that Samuel–Kings and Chronicles both drew upon an independent, shared source, which they each shaped in different ways, has not found wide acceptance (*Kings without Privilege: David and Moses in the Story of the Bible's Kings* [Edinburgh: T. & T. Clark, 1994]).

past for its own sake, for reading and remembering, while taking a soft brush to it in order to touch it up and fill in the gaps where necessary.

I think it important to recognize that in the late Persian period Yehud, there was a need to forge a new form of community identity under changed political circumstances, when there were no clear indigenous models within Israel's literature to create a new form of political community. Earlier, the Deuteronomistic Historian had sought to grant the monarch complete authority over matters of cult and Temple, despite the absence of precedent for such a move in Deuteronomy, his ostensible source.[38] In the context of the later Persian period, the Chronicler confronted a still more serious problem in seeking divine warrant for his attempt to configure the postexilic Judean polity as a Davidide-led royal temple state following contemporary Achaemenid models. Neither the Pentateuch (the ostensible legal foundation of the postexilic theocracy) nor the Deuteronomistic History (the Chronicler's ostensible historiographic source) sufficed: pentateuchal law envisaged no cultic role for the monarch (Deut 17:14–20) and the Deuteronomistic History reflected the needs of an exilic community requiring a justification for the destruction and assurance that the history of the nation had not come to an abrupt end. The Chronicler's aim, in contrast, was

[38] Gary N. Knoppers, "The Deuteronomist and the Deuteronomic Law of the King: A Reexamination of a Relationship," *ZAW* 108 (1996): 329–46; idem, "Rethinking the Relationship between Deuteronomy and the Deuteronomistic History: The Case of Kings," *CBQ* 63 (2001): 393–415; Bernard M. Levinson, "The Reconceptualization of Kingship in Deuteronomy and the Deuteronomistic History's Transformation of Torah," *VT* 51 (2001): 511–34.

to provide a practical blueprint for the reconstruction of the Second Commonwealth. Nevertheless, to claim continuity with past conventions of cultus and monarchy, the Chronicler rewrote his sources in light of the new program.

Integrating the literary technique and the contemporizing agenda, Gary N. Knoppers productively invokes an analogy to the phenomenon of rewritten Bible, a genre more normally associated with the Dead Sea Scrolls and the book of Jubilees:

> Such works take as a point of departure an earlier biblical book or collection of books. They select from, interpret, comment on, and expand portions of a particular biblical book (or group of books), addressing obscurities, contradictions, and other perceived problems with the source text. Rewritten Bible texts normally emulate the form of the source text and follow it sequentially. The major intention of such works seems to be to provide a coherent interpretive reading of the biblical text.[39]

This model is, of course, directly relevant to the study of inner-biblical exegesis: here the new composition uses an older composition as its literary point of departure. Knoppers also addresses the function of the new composition:

> [T]here is something to be said for viewing Chronicles as a second national epic. Chronicles was composed not necessarily as a replacement of, but as an alternative to the primary history. . . . Indeed, the Chronicler's work may have had an effect on how these older works were interpreted by some readers. After reading the Chronicler's composition and its selective incorporation of earlier writings, ancient

39 Knoppers, *1 Chronicles 1–9*, 130.

readers may have understood those earlier writings differently. By the same token, the author's skillful reuse, reinterpretation, rearrangement, and major supplementation of sections within the primary history all conspire to create a very different work.... The new traditions incorporated within the body of the text, coupled with the reworking of selections from older biblical texts, contribute to the creation of a new literary work that is designed to suit the writer's own times and interests in the Second Commonwealth.[40]

Although Knoppers is careful not to claim any notion of simple replacement, the salient issue is that Chronicles is here understood to be an autonomous work that now stands independently. The past, as historical memory but also as text, is reinterpreted, reordered, rewritten, and supplemented to serve the present needs of the community.

Since a number of superb commentaries have recently been completed, the reader is encouraged to explore the range of issues raised by the Chronicler independently. JAPHET's 1991 volume is a valuable English translation of a Hebrew original that helped introduce a new perspective to the study of Chronicles in its relationship to Samuel and Kings. She demonstrates the extent to which the Chronicler exegetically transforms his literary sources by revising earlier notions of divine agency or morality with later conceptions. She emphasizes the extent to which the Chronicler was historiographer, thinker, and author. Her commentary integrates these perspectives with a systematic study of the book as a whole, with particular attention to matters of historiography and its value as an historical source. KALIMI

40 Knoppers, *1 Chronicles 1–9*, 133–34.

identifies the specific literary techniques employed in the reuse of the Chronicler's source material. The volumes by Bendavid (in Hebrew) or Endres (in English) align the texts of Chronicles and Samuel–Kings alongside each other, in parallel columns, highlighting points of comparison, contrast, and gaps, permitting the reader to see the literary activity of the Chronicler in action. Aside from its attention to matters of textual criticism, the commentary by Knoppers is especially rich in its attention to the history of the Samaritan community and its relevance to Second Temple literature and history. Klein's commentary in the prestigious Hermeneia series brings together a lifetime of scholarship on Chronicles. The recent article by Jonker surveys the different approaches scholars have taken to understanding the function of Chronicles; the author makes fascinating analogies to postapartheid South Africa and the need to prepare a "reforming history" that reinterprets the past to create a new communal identity in the present.

Author Index

The names of authors writing before 1800 C.E. are set in small caps. Both text and footnotes are indexed here. References to notes in the main text take the form of 4n5; references to those in the Foreword take the form of x n3 (thus adding a space to distinguish the note number from the page number, which is given in Roman numerals). Locators in bold indicate authors discussed in chapter 6, the bibliographic essay.

Subject Index

Index of Scriptural and Other Sources

Hebrew Bible/Old Testament

CPSIA information can be obtained at www.ICGtesting.com
Printed in the USA
BVOW070416040112

279731BV00001B/46/P